'TIL THE RIVER RUNS DRY

ONE WOMAN'S JOURNEY

BY R.E.M. WILLIS

PREFACE

In a way, divorce was worse than an actual death. All I could focus on was the huge loss I'd suffered. Only he was still out there, but he did not want me. I was not good enough. "Was I good enough for anyone else?" I asked the gray cloudy sky above.

It was easy convincing myself there was no one out there for me. But, what now? Should I give up my purpose? What was the point of living a life I never imagined or asked for?

As a young girl, I felt I had a destiny. At nine years old, I could foresee my future. I would be a teacher, coach and a mom. Through different events in my life I began to put together a plan. This was MY plan. That was my first mistake. As life revealed itself to me, I realized I had to be more open to God's calling. It was not always convenient, and it did not seem to go along with MY plan. Finally, I realized I had no control over my life and that indeed it was not my plan at all. The only way to have any resemblance of order is to submit to the maker of all heaven and earth. I had to become more open to his will and in the quiet, listen. The pages that follow are about a young girl and how she gained control of her life by letting go of it. When we think we have accomplished our purpose there is another one waiting. Life continues if you believe. Believe in God, believe in self, and allow God to take over and it will happen His way in His time. God has plans for us until the river runs dry. The river still runs in my life, and this vessel sails on.

DEDICATION

First and foremost, I want to thank God for all my blessings and the strength to never give up. I have many blessings; included are my family and our friends, Mike and Mary. I thank Garth Brooks for his music. I thank all those people that I know and don't know that have encouraged me in thoughts and prayers. Thanks to my husband, Kent, who was hand-picked by God for me and is my rock and forever love. I especially appreciate the help from Melba Stohlhand and Carol McCleod. Thanks to the readers of this book and I hope one person might see something that will someway help make this voyage called life a little more manageable.

BIOGRAPHY

R.E.M. Willis was raised in a small Missouri town. She spent forty-five years teaching and coaching. She was also a very active speaker for Teens Encounter Christ and has been a speaker at women's conferences and cheer coach conventions. She served on the state cheer board in Oklahoma for approximately eighteen years and spent two years on the State Cheer Advisory Board. She has organized All-Region Tryouts and served as an All-State judge for eighteen years. During her coaching career she was honored by being chosen East All-state Coach in 2001, Region 3 Coach of the year in 2005 and the Oklahoma Cheer Coach of the year in 2006. At the end of her career in 2017, she was chosen one of the six National Finalists for Coach of the Year in Special Sports, which included bowling, cheer, field hockey etc. This award was given by the National High School Athletic Coaches Association.

CHAPTER ONE
~Thoughts~

Life tends to cause people to lose their way. We begin to doubt our beliefs and turn in a direction that stifles who we're meant to become. It comes after setbacks and even times when we feel we are doing everything right. The unforeseen is a gift helping one find their purpose. It does not always just fall in your lap. Many prayers ask for what you want out of life and are not directed to God's purpose. Throughout my days on this planet, new challenges have been raised without me giving much thought about the ultimate outcome or praying to seek God's guidance. I have learned, as much as we like to be in control, we are not. God has ways of getting your attention. His teaching moments are not always positive. It seems many times they are painful. Some people just want to give up. Some want to bury their heads in the sand. And there are others that try to face these good or bad times straight on without understanding how a moment in time can change your entire life. Learning to hold on during life's rollercoaster ride is truly a gift from God. No one is ever promised an easy life and I believe our society needs to learn how to weather the storms as well as sunshiny days. I discovered this truth early on. Through one challenge and then another, I thanked God and learned my lessons.

Several years ago, I sat on a bluff, staring off into space, I scanned the beautiful lush fall forest below. Breathing deep, the fall scent was in the air. The golds and browns, and especially the oranges made my heart and my mind wander back in time.

As mental notes were made, I recalled when my story first began. I was just nine years old when my thoughts began to foresee what God had planned for me.

Sitting in front of our black and white television console, President Kennedy spoke with passion and conviction when, he said "Ask not what your country can do for you, ask what you can do for your country." This advice set my life in motion to become who I am today. At that moment in time, on my hardwood floor in a small Missouri town, my life was set, or so I thought.

Since fourth grade, I wanted to become a teacher and coach. These two desires settled in my heart. MY plan was to put these desires into motion. A big family was also in my future dreams. I even looked through the Sears catalog and picked out the husband and kids I wanted.

My mom and dad had been great role models. As factory workers we did not have a lot, but we had plenty of love. My two brothers from my mother's first marriage were older, so in many ways after I entered school, I was an only child. Even though we were a blended family, it never really felt like it.

When I was in first grade, my youngest older brother Jim was a senior. I depended on him because he was my ride to school and was my protector. He made sure the older kids did not bug me. It didn't hurt that he was a popular athlete. He was an awesome basketball player known by the nickname "Curly," because of his big brown eyes and curly eyelashes. I felt a swell of pride when I watched him play basketball. My older brother, Denny, graduated before I entered school. He was an athlete and a musician. He sure could sing and spent many hours on the guitar and singing the latest Hank William's songs. I especially loved watching him in the senior class play. He played a singing cowboy.

While in fourth grade, we moved into our new house and my dad in time got a new job in another town about twenty miles away. He drove back and forth for a while, but when I turned sixteen, we moved to Rolla. This required my mom to get a new job and me to attend a new school.

In elementary school, following in the footsteps of my brothers, I played every sport I could. In my mind, athletics kept me in good shape and would help me with scholarships later. They also kept me very busy. Organization became important to me and by the time I reached my freshman year in high school, my future was set. The plan was simple. I would go to college, get a degree to become a teacher and coach, and meet a husband along the way. Those who knew me understood I always had a plan and a dream.

But moving to another town in the middle of my high school career was going to be a challenge. I had been in the same school since kindergarten. My friends were my life. Not knowing anyone in the new school made me very nervous and I felt lost on the first day. Also, a new teaching staff frightened me. This huge adjustment made me a little sick to my stomach. Entering the doors of the high school was one of the most difficult times of my life, up until that moment.

After a time of adjustment, finding new friends and being part of a new high school did not seem as daunting. The new school though different was also great. Since it was a school in our Conference, we had played them in all sports. Being an athlete was a big help. The coaches knew me. I was welcomed with open arms. Making good grades was important to me as well as fostering good people skills. Working and playing hard was just a part of me. In my old school, I was in the yearbook court and was part of the FFA royalty at my new school. My friends were great. I cheered, played volleyball and softball. Being named the most valuable player in both volleyball and softball was a goal reached. My senior year I was voted best spiker on the volleyball team and I was voted most athletic by my senior class. I was counting on scholarships and grants etc., to go to college. It worked.

I soon felt life was once again great and I had the world by the tail. I decided my future would continue just like my past had been (easy, and as planned). I had known nothing else. Was I mistaken? My real story had yet to unfold.

CHAPTER TWO
~Beginning a New Journey~

It was mid-August and I was preparing to go to the second largest college in Missouri. At the time it was SMS in Springfield. I was from a town of about 2,000 people. Arriving on campus was awe inspiring. Talk about a little fish in a big pond, it was more like a small goldfish in the ocean. My first class had over 250 students in it. There were more students in that one class than my whole first high school. I will never forget the first words my professor spoke. He said, "Look to the right, now, look to your left. Two of you will have dropped this class by next week." Interpretation, this class was going to be one of the hardest challenges I had ever imagined. I did not know if I would be one of those left. I felt a little dizzy, my ears were ringing, and suddenly I was a little sick. Sweat was rolling down my neck. Am I going to pass out? Passing out had never been a thing for me. Oh well, maybe once, when cheering at a very close basketball game. It was a small gym with very small windows. The gym was full of excitement but claustrophobic with a smell of sweat permeating the air. The last thing I recalled was jumping to do a toe touch. I came to with something stuffed under my nose and I was lying on the floor with several faces staring down at me. When my brain started working again, I could only think about how it must have looked when I hit the floor like a sack of potatoes. Embarrassing does not even cover it. As time passed, it became a funny story to tell. As my mind came back to the professor and his words, I knew I had to decide what I was going to do. Was I going to do what it takes or give up? My athletic training never allowed me to think about giving up. So, I decided to just do well. It seemed simple enough. Not really.

The professor was right. Many dropped out. The class became a third of its original size. Many students were in a sorority or fraternity. I was not part of Greek life and had no desire to be. One of the problems I had was competing with pledges to fraternities that had copies of former tests given by the professor and saved by the fraternity or sorority in their house files. This in my mind gave them a great advantage. It was difficult seeing people score much higher on tests than me. Many times, they did not even take notes. I learned they had copies of them too. Oh well, I ended up with a B+ which I had earned on my own. I was proud of my accomplishment.

After adjusting to the initial shock of a huge university, I started looking at certain areas of the SMS campus. The science building, the social studies building, the math building and the physical education building were the only buildings I needed to navigate to and from. Approved housing was about one block from campus. This housing was set up for students who could not be housed in the dorms. There were too many freshmen and too few dorm rooms. In a way, I was lucky because the rules were not as stringent as dorm rules. There were four girls in our apartment. Three of the girls were from St. Louis and, of course, me. All of them were smokers but me. It was cool and sophisticated in 1969. I must admit I felt somewhat to be the country bumpkin. If you recall, I had made up my mind at age nine to be a teacher/coach. I really did not have a desire to fit in any certain group but just wanted to have good relationships with all people. I did however feel I would give smoking a chance. It seemed soothing for my roommates. So, I bought a pack of Winston's for 35 cents. It was a wasted effort. I did not like the taste and it did not sooth my nerves. It made me cough. Also, my clothes and hair stunk like cigarette smoke. What was this attraction? My roommates said you just had to get used to it. Anything I had to get used to was not my idea of something I should do. So, after two days, I gave my smokes to my roommate. So for me, it was one of the best 35 cent investments of my life. Drinking was another experiment. I found out I was not a person that held my liquor. Two drinks and I went to sleep. So, this two-drink limit has pretty much followed me through life. To this day, I can't understand how people can get so drunk they do things they cannot recollect. I think this was God's way of keeping me focused. Drugs were everywhere on campus in the late 60s and 70s. I was at a school where pot could be smelled in the halls of the buildings that I attended class in each day. I had a psychology class that included a trip to a drug rehab ward. We were to observe the behavior of the drug addicts. I saw one man trying to dig through a wall to escape the ward. His hands were bloody and an orderly came in and put a straitjacket on him so he would not literally dig until his fingers were bloody and deformed. This again was God working because after witnessing this, I wanted absolutely nothing to do with drugs. After all, we were told pot was a gateway drug. No, I never even experimented.

My English class was one of my favorites. The professor was so "cool." Every other word that poured easily from his mouth, I considered forbidden. My sheltered ears blushed. He was so interesting, and I was enamored with his sophistication. He said he was going to help us become writers. I knew this was going to be a great class, because it was much smaller than the history class mentioned above, only forty students and I had captured a front row seat. I always loved writing and had done well in high school. On the first day, our first assignment was to write about a person who had influenced our life the most. I picked Jesus.

One would think that was a great choice. Writing about my faith and the difference it had made for me seemed like a natural thing. It had been at a revival in our local First Baptist Church. After a week of singing wonderful hymns, listening to a young vibrant preacher, I felt a major tug in my chest. It would not go away. I needed to follow my heart. I found myself walking to the front and shaking the preacher's hand. On the following Sunday, all those that had come forward during the revival were baptized. I was a new person, free of sin. My life would forever be changed. My new faith foundation became very important to me. My essay was sure to get an A or B. The next week the essays were handed back. I was so excited to get the grade. I stared at the grade in disbelief. A big fat D minus was on the paper in red ink. The pages were riddled with red marks. What? I had never gotten a D let alone a D minus. I was embarrassed and began to look around. I saw that most of the other students had similar looks of disbelief on their faces as well. After finishing handing out the papers, the professor wrote on the board the number of A's - 0, B's - 0, C's - 0, D's - 2 and F's - 38. Confused and glancing around, I did not know how to react. Should I be happy for the D minus? Who else got a D? In the beginning, the professor knocked us down a bit and spent the semester building us back up. So, all in all, it was a humbling experience, however, the professor knew exactly how to motivate his students. He was one of the best.

Starting out as a Physical Education major, I had to take several science classes. I had taken biology in high school, but it was not my favorite. Approaching my first zoology class, I did not realize how much it would change my life and upset my plan. We had class three days a week and lab two days a week. The lab was small enough that the professor could give the students individual attention. However, when we had to pith a frog and split it open to see how the frog's organs worked, there were plenty of people that needed help. Just in case you have never pithed a frog, to pith is to pierce or sever the spinal cord of an animal, in this case a frog, to immobilize it. My dissection of a dead worm in high school did not in any way prepare me for this task. The instructions were to put a live frog's head between my ring finger and middle finger on my left hand. Next, take the body between my middle finger and index finger allowing the legs to dangle between my index finger and thumb. Next, take a dissection probe inserting it into the brain of the frog forcing it to be paralyzed. This allows the student to watch the inner workings of the frog. What, I had to cripple a living being? This act was not in me. After trying to muster up enough courage and stomach to do this, I realized in my wildest dreams, I could not do it. Just about that time another student asked if I needed help. I said sure. He was cute and seemed to know what he was doing. So, the frog was pithed, and phone numbers exchanged. I was totally nauseous. In a few days we decided to get together.

CHAPTER THREE
~Decisions Made in Haste
Can Change Your Life Forever~

Just a week or so after we had pithed the frog, I was injured in my gymnastics class. I collided with a student in midair. We were being taught to do a headspring. This is not a safe move and has been made illegal in many classes. At the same time I sprang forward a guy about twice my size came flying through the air, and "KaBlam," I was projected back and landed on my head. My neck popped. It was a horrible sound. I was afraid to move, and I just knew my neck was broken. My coach saw what happened and rushed to my aid. He decided it should be checked out. An ambulance pulled up outside of the gym, sirens blaring. After being placed on a board with my head and neck immobilized, I was taken to the emergency room. x-rays were done and it was found that my neck had an S-shape. My head ached and throbbed. My neck had no movement without great pain and I also had a concussion. It was decided nothing was broken. Loaded up with pain medication and muscle relaxers, I was sent home. To this day I still have problems with this neck injury. But really it is the least of my pain today. My new lab friend stepped up to take care of me. My parents came and checked on me and they were satisfied that everything was under control. Listening to the doctor was very important for my recovery. No physical education classes for a year or so. This meant a change of my major field or be a year behind. History and social studies were always my favorite classes in high school. I changed my major to Comprehensive Social Science. With this change, I could now take geology to satisfy my science requirements.

At least I would not have to kill any rocks or gems. The class was enjoyable, and I found it helpful in my geography classes. What about coaching? Understanding now a little more how God works, the coaching came with a purpose in His time.

My friends at home were getting married in rapid succession. I felt a little left out. Since it was 1969, it was common to get married by twenty or so. I had several boyfriends in high school but after leaving for college nothing really continued. I dated a few boys I knew from high school in college but nothing even close to serious resulted. I guess I had a mindset of what I wanted. After the lab friend stepped up, we began to date. He was not exactly what I wanted, but he seemed like a good guy with ambition. It became serious quickly. I jumped the gun so to speak. After a whirlwind-paced courtship, we decided to get married. We were both in college and had three years left to go. Timing was not the best and of course, we were so young, just eighteen. My parents questioned me about our decision. My mother especially felt uneasy about our age. I am sure his parents did the same. But of course, we thought we knew what was best for us. I was too eager to begin My Perfect Life.

Staying in school was a challenge but we did and kept good GPAs. We were always on at least the Dean's list and sometimes the President's. We did not have much time to party or get into trouble. Between part-time jobs and studying, there were not enough hours in the day. My worst semester was my first. Because of my injury, all I had to do was attend classes and I was assured a C. We graduated on schedule, but we had some very rough times.

At first things seemed great. We were, however, POOR

college students. We did not even have a car. Luckily, we lived close to campus and really did not need one. The grocery store was a block away. Bicycles were the answer. So, our life consisted of getting together with friends, working on campus, studying and going to class. This was a very busy life. When we wanted to go home, we could usually catch a ride with people who lived in our hometowns, and our parents made trips to see us.

We then realized for summer jobs we would have to have a vehicle to get to work. We both loved nature and the great outdoors. We decided to see if we could get jobs with the U.S. Forest Service. We were successful and moved for the summer to Southeastern Missouri. It was a beautiful part of the state and a wonderful experience. These dream jobs transformed into part-time jobs for the next three years. We loved our work and we kept on task with our classes. I am not saying there were no problems. There were. About three and a half years into the marriage, my husband became very verbally abusive. He felt he had been pushed into the marriage. We were also having money issues. Tension over classes, papers, and tests promoted stress. He would say things in anger that would break my heart. Some signs of infidelity began to surface but I would not accept that possibility.

We had purchased a house in his hometown. It was about an hour from SMS. It was a good buy, but it was two hours a day on the road. This added to the stressful student life. Since we lived very close to his family, I began to understand my husband's abusive language. The exchanges between his parents and his siblings seemed quite abrupt. Remember, my childhood was almost like a fairytale. My life experience had not really prepared me for this type of communication.

We began to realize the drive each day was a bit much. Plus, if a job was available after graduation that was close to campus, it would be the most logical choice. Once graduated, I applied for many jobs and was offered a teaching job just twelve miles from the university. My husband was still completing some graduate work, so we decided to sell our house and purchase a mobile home. We bought a very nice mobile home in our price range, had it transported and set up in a mobile home park on the south side of Springfield, which was even closer to my job. This worked out great for a while. I found some other teachers that were driving every day to my school, so I became part of a carpool. We so far were making it with only one car being on the road. It later became obvious that we would need to add a second car. My experience in cheer, gymnastics, and dance made it a good fit to become a cheer coach. The requirements were not as stringent as other sports. Cheer was not considered a sport in 1973. Over the years, however, it has evolved into a sport in most states. Especially those that have high school competitive cheer and stunt. I did not realize that this choice to do cheer was going to become a major part of my professional life and my life's purpose. I developed strong feelings about young women and their futures. I believed I could help them become strong independent adults. This became my mission, my purpose, my life.

It was expensive maintaining two cars, but it helped my spouse concentrate on his master's degree. However, cheerleading was also very time consuming. We cheered for football and basketball, and of course, there were practices. I did have a co-coach. Since there were no competitions, there were no lengthy practices after school. The games could be as many as three a week. My co-coach who had been a college cheerleader was great. He had been part of a co-ed squad. His wife had actually cheered with him. We decided to add what we called stuntmen which added practice time.

It was during this first year of teaching and coaching that my husband announced he would have to spend more time at the university. Meanwhile, I was working two jobs putting him through graduate school. As time went on, signs of infidelity surfaced again. More and more there were late nights. We began to grow apart and spent very little time together. He began to pick at me. "You are getting a fat belly," he would say. His insults became more and more pointed and he managed to make me feel unworthy of the life as I had imagined it. Each day it seemed worse and worse. How could I have any pride in myself when my own husband thought I needed to lose weight? I weighed 145 lbs. at 5 feet 8 1/2 inches. It became too much, so during the summer, I left him. It became evident that he had indeed cheated on me with one of my very best friends. I felt so betrayed. I had lost my trust in friendships and my husband. My job was important to me, so I had to figure out where I was going to live when school started again. Leaving was my only option. I was not going to support my husband, his girlfriends and his graduate school. Just as I had found a small apartment in the same town as my school, I got a phone call from my husband begging me to come home. He said he wanted me back and was crying. He said he had made a horrible mistake. He begged for forgiveness, so I agreed to come home to talk things out and try to put our marriage back together again. As I went back to the trailer, my thoughts were full of uncertainty and fear of how things would be.

At first, he welcomed me back and seemed to be trying hard to make amends. He effectively convinced me things would be different. He made an effort to curb the hateful rhetoric. I felt better about our future. So, we decided that we needed to live closer to school and my job. We found a lovely trailer park. It was just a mile and a half from school. In the long run it would save money. The lot rent was less, and we would save on gas money. My husband decided to see if he could find another student that attended the university, so they could share rides. He soon found a rider.

Since being married, I had pretty much pulled away from my church upbringing. I did continue to pray but my prayer life was inconsistent. My hopes and plans were to start a family. The doctor unexpectedly told me that it would be difficult for me to conceive. My uterus was tilted, and my periods were irregular. There was still hope that I could, but the timing was not good. My husband wanted to get his doctorate. This meant my dream family would have to wait for at least two, maybe even three more years. Someone had to have a job. As time went on, I began to feel used. I was a paycheck and not much more. He did have a job, but my check pretty much paid the bills. The verbal abuse started again, and again I felt worthless. Many people think physical abuse is the only kind of abuse that counts. Verbal abuse can be just as damaging to the soul as physical abuse can be to the body. Trying to hold things together, I convinced myself that when he finished his doctorate, I would get my master's degree and things would be a lot better. Little did I know that the chance to get my MA in Education would not be any time soon.

In the spring, my spouse was offered a fellowship to continue his education which would result in a doctorate. One of the things that had attracted me to him was his intelligence. I wanted someone I could talk to about the world, life, etc. I began to look back over our years together and wondered if I should follow him to Chicago and find a job and continue to be the supportive wife. We made the decision to move. I turned in my resignation and prepared for the new life. As I cleaned out my classroom, I realized how much I was going to miss my school, my students, and my colleagues. Maybe a fresh start in a new city was what we needed. Chicago was a big place, but we would live in a nearby suburb, Oak Park. I felt I had made the right decision. The move would be one more giant step to save this union.

CHAPTER FOUR
~Life Can Turn on a Dime~

Before we moved to Oak Park, my husband came home one evening and started yelling again. What more could I do to be supportive? I had given up my job and was searching for a new job in the Chicago area. He decided to go to Chicago alone. What? Then he went too far. His words were even worse than usual. Something inside of me was done. I went to our room, dug in the back of the closet and pulled out a suitcase and packed it. He asked what I was doing. I simply said "leaving." He began to shout saying I would be back. He also told me that he and his "rider" had been having an affair. I felt sick like I was going to throw up. The rider was one of my student's sister. The first thing that crossed my mind was how many people in this small town and school system knew. I turned to go out the door. The last words he spoke on that night I will never forget. "You will be back. You are just like a puppy. I can kick you and mistreat you, but YOU will come back, you will be back." I had given him a second chance. I could not come back. "NO, I WILL NOT!"

Walking to the trunk of my car, I threw my suitcase in and knew in my heart I would never come back to this place. As I sat down in my Ford Pinto and started it up, I had to decide where I was going. I had $100 in my purse after pulling money from the bank for groceries and I had a full tank of gas. I pulled over at the first phonebooth. Cell phones were not yet invented. I made a collect call to my mom and dad. My mom accepted the charges. I told her I was jobless and had $100 to my name, also, I had to divorce my husband. Without hesitation she said, "Head home." That is what I did.

CHAPTER FIVE
~WORN OUT AND DREAM GONE~

From 18 years old to 25 brought conflict and some extremely tough times. My life was heading in the wrong direction. I really thought I had done everything right. I guess I did something right because his family seemed to support me. I was lost and my life seemed in shambles. Why had it deviated from my plan? It was all laid out. Good plans; finish high school with good grades, get scholarships, finish college, get married along the way, and find a teaching/coaching job, and live happily ever after. What had happened? It was all my fault.

I came back home to my mom and dad's. I wanted to find a job close by that needed a cheer coach. My first job had shown me that cheer was a passion of mine. Believe it or not cheer coaches were not that abundant. In 1976, many young female teachers were just told if you want the job, you will have to supervise the cheerleaders. Remember, most of these young teachers were approximately 22 years old. Many had to take one class to coach cheer and that was their professional training. They sometimes were not much more mature than the teenagers they were working with. Believe it or not, three to four years was about all a new coach could handle. This means they were not quite versed in how to deal with the raging hormones of the girls. As a sponsor, working with the parents could sometimes be a challenge, to say the least. Plus, they themselves were coming into their own in a new career. I was trained and wanted to coach cheer. I was sort of an oddity. I knew my challenge was to work to help teenage girls. My job was to help them understand that there are many different types of abuse. Physical abuse is not the only kind. Sexual abuse and psychological abuse many times were not, and are still not, as easily recognizable. I wanted to help young girls to become independent women and follow their dreams.

Much of my alone time was spent in thought about what my contribution was to my failed marriage. One day maybe I would understand why this time of my life was necessary to lead to the outcome God wanted for me. But, in the meanwhile, I took it one day at a time.

By this time, I was twenty-five years old. Divorced, no job, now what do I do? First, I needed to find a way to support myself. God and JFK had made it clear I was to teach. The search for a teaching position was something that helped me focus on other things beside my divorce. Thank goodness teaching was my career field. I had a part of my plan still intact. Yes, I was praying. I was asking, what now and what about the family I was supposed to have? My mind would drift back to my younger years and remember the longing for a family. This was not in the past. I still needed to be a mom. Twenty-five is young and today many people don't even think about marriage until much later. But it was a different time. All my high school friends were married and were having children. So, as I said, finding another job kept me from feeling sorry for myself. I was living with my parents because obviously I had no money. I wanted to find the right position for me and my future. I could not go back to my first job because my position had been filled. I wanted to stay close to my hometown this time. After searching all the area schools, I found an available job in a small district about twenty miles from my parents' house, Newburg High School.

I had received some great advice from a counselor in college to get qualified in more than one area. So, after my injury, I made a decision to major in comprehensive social sciences and minor in English. This decision helped me to be qualified for several classes. I could teach and was certified in American history, world history, government, geography, psychology, and sociology grades nine through twelve, and in grades seven through nine, English was also on my teaching certification. This led to a job offer to teach English to grades seven through nine. At this point my next move would be to find a place to live.

While relocating to Rolla, the mobile home I had with my ex-husband sold, which gave me some operating money. My car was doing fine, so the search began for an apartment. It had to be something within my means. Also, I had no furniture or kitchen utensils, just clothes and shoes etc. I found a two-bedroom apartment that would be perfect. Garage sales were my source for cheap furnishings. My mom cleaned out her cabinets of odds and ends. So, with a skillet and two saucepans, plus four cups, four plates, four bowls, four glasses and silverware service for four, I started my new kitchen. I had two towels and washcloths, plus a set of sheets for a full bed. The stove and refrigerator were provided. I was set. My living room, including a television, was furnished for less than $250. I purchased a dining table and chairs for $75, and my mother gave me my bed and dresser from high school. Another find was a desk and a twin rollaway bed for the extra room. This made a great office and an extra bedroom. Enough money was left to make it to my first paycheck. We rounded up old friends to help move my stuff out of my mom and dad's basement. After all were placed inside, it became my new home. School started in a week, so I had a little time left to settle in before I had to hit the ground running.

Nervous, new people, new boss, new town and just starting again were hurdles before me. I waved at the neighbors as I left my apartment as they were getting into their car. They were two sisters also starting a new job. Driving to school, the views of the the hills were beautiful. After parking my car in the teachers' lot, I walked inside. Looking around at all the new faces, my heart was pounding and felt like it was going to jump out of my chest. Finding an open seat at the general meeting, I introduced myself. My heart rate slowed as I relaxed a bit.

After our meeting was over, all the teachers and staff went to their respective rooms to get ready for the kids the next day. Numbering books, setting up role sheets, writing lesson plans and doing bulletin boards filled the afternoon.

I was teaching Junior High English and found myself teaching in the old elementary building upstairs. At my previous school I had taught high school only. Praying to find the right job and meet the right people had been a daily request. Cheer was part of my duties, so I needed to meet the other coach. It was going to be a guy. I had worked with a guy at my first school and it worked out great. Squaring my shoulders and hoping for the best, I entered his room and I had hit the jackpot. He was truly a nice guy. He was married and had a baby on the way. I had no idea on that first day of our meeting that he and his wife would become my lifeline and my true forever friends. Forever friends are very hard to find, and they are the ones held in your heart.It was not too long before this school felt like home. Oh yes, and the two neighbors that I waved at the first day, they taught at the same school. We shared rides and saved a lot of money on gas. The Lord had done just what I had asked, the right people and the right job. Still, my love for my future family did not come to fruition. I did not understand why the family I dreamed of was nowhere in sight. The longing for children and a husband did not go away. I was almost twenty-six and my divorce had just become final. The day of the divorce was the last time I saw my first husband. For some reason he had a need to tell me he would always love me, and we had just been too young. Yes, we had been. I thought as years passed, I would understand how God's plan was served by this. I could not see how it had served MY plan.

CHAPTER SIX
~God's Plan Continues, Not Mine~

The students were what I expected for a small rural school. For the most part, they were nice kids and had been taught to respect teachers. So, the job was very enjoyable. The families in the area were very poor for the most part. The district was considered a depressed area, which means each year I worked at this school canceled a part of any left-over student debt. I ended up owing nothing. A true blessing was granted.

The cheer program was very small. There were six to eight girls. My co-coach and I decided to add what we called "stuntmen," male cheerleaders. We could not have possibly called them cheerleaders in rural Missouri. Again, this is what we had done in my former school. It raised school spirit and we could do stunts that they had never been able to do before. My new school did not have football, so we had plenty of time to teach stunts and get them ready for basketball. The other coach and I learned some of the partner stunts to teach. It was fun, but since he had been in the army and had not done anything like this before, we had some funny moments. It was not unusual for his wife to be present when we learned the stunts on the stage of the old gym. Once while practicing a stunt, he lifted me to his shoulders. A little crisp unexpected "wootie pootie" popped out from my stunt partner. Mary started laughing on the floor. As mentioned before, she was very pregnant. She was on her back, holding her belly and rolling side to side. This was her version of rolling with laughter. Mike and I tried to ignore it, but we looked at each other and laughed until we cried. Any pretense of saving face was totally lost in that moment. We were forming a very special relationship. Mike and Mary became family.

My co-coach became my confidant. His wife and I became great friends. I have never had friends like these. Later I knew without a doubt that God had put them in my life for a very important purpose, to save me from my pity party. They introduced me to others and helped me find my way back to church. I really needed a church family, people I could talk to and figured out I was not the only person going through deep hurt.

Feeling like a third wheel was okay because soon others became part of our friendship group. We really enjoyed working together and sharing time outside of work. I had no idea what an important part of God's plan these two friends would become.

As time passed, we spent more and more time together. Weekends were filled with cookouts and talks into the night about life, religion, and the world around us. After six months, I began to think about dating again. No one I knew really was who I was looking for. Most of my friends were married. I was going to be more careful this time. One was too old, another too young, one did not have much of a personality, and finally one was the right age with a great job but was not for me. None of these guys were right. No chemistry and very few things in common. What did I want? I wanted a Christian, tall, athletic, loving man that wanted kids. Was that too much to ask?

My faith had again become very important to me. My new friends were solid in their faith and all the long talks had brought Christ back into my life. I was 5 feet 8 1/2 inches and my first husband was about 5 feet 10 inches. I never really dated anyone that short before, because I liked feeling small sometimes. Marriage and motherhood were still on my heart. This emptiness ever present led me to pray about this part of my plan. I prayed every day for the life I had seen as a young child. However, nothing seemed to be fitting into my plan. Notice I keep referring to my future as MY PLAN. First mistake. It was God's plan for me, not MY PLAN.

As the year went by, I became very involved with my students and cheerleaders. One thing I knew for sure was to make certain my students understood their worth. Still feeling inferior because of the words that had been spoken to break my spirit, the confident person I had once been was still emotionally bruised. It seemed my very soul was damaged. How could anyone want me now? I felt to be a "has been." I wasn't good enough for my first husband. What made me think I could be with anyone else? My friends saw my loneliness and sadness. They tried very hard to bolster my spirits. Slowly, but surely, my confidence began to come back. Still I was super critical of myself. I even asked Mike if I was worthy of another relationship. He said, "of course you are." At one time, he thought one of his friends might be good for me. I still felt so lost and needed to share my life with someone. I began to look at divorce in a different light. In a way, divorce was worse than an actual death. At least in death the person would be gone. One would not wonder about them and their new life. Was he happy now or was he hurting too? Why did I still yearn for children? What now? Should I give up my purpose? I would continue working with the kids at school and at least work toward that part of my dream life.

CHAPTER SEVEN
~And, There He was~

Just as my heart was about to give up on love, I went to a restaurant/pub after a game with Mike and Mary. There was a dance floor and music. I had always loved to dance but was fine with only watching and snacking. This was a full-blown disco-era pub. It had a disco ball and all the strobe lights. My friends and I were talking and enjoying the music when a man came up to our table and asked me if I wanted to dance. I thought, "What the heck?" He was tall, 6 foot 4 inches, had a shaggy blond haircut, and was quite good looking. He looked like he enjoyed dancing as much as I did. He was pretty good, and I started feeling comfortable. We danced every dance after that until the place closed. He asked to take me home and I decided it would be fine. As we drove to my apartment, I found out he was a student at the local university. He was older because he too had gone through a divorce and decided to finish his education to become an engineer. We agreed to see each other again. In our conversation, he mentioned he attended the same church as Mike and Mary. I thought I might go to see sometime if he was there. As it turned out I went the following Sunday.

The church was very full, so we had to sit in the balcony, or choir loft. As communion was being offered, I watched to see if I saw the back of his head. Yes, I saw him! I joined Mike and Mary for lunch after church. Later that afternoon the phone rang, and it was him wanting to know if we could get together. We set a date and time. He seemed excited and I felt a fluttery feeling in my stomach. He arrived on time and I had fixed dinner. It was nothing big, just burgers, chips, and ice cream for dessert. We spent the rest of the evening talking. We learned so much about each other. I found out he had been diagnosed as a manic/depressive. He took medication that totally controlled his symptoms. He had no children and would probably never be able to father a child, due to an accident when he was younger. For some reason this was not a huge red flag for me, because I had just found out that I would most likely never conceive due to female problems. I had undergone two DNCs by this time. I really liked this guy and decided to continue seeing him to see where it would lead.

He continued working on his degree and I continued teaching. After the spring semester, he was offered a job and decided to take it so we could think more about our future. He would continue taking courses as he could. As time passed our friendship developed into much more. He asked if I would be interested in marriage? At first, I was a little hesitant. Maybe a little more time would help. I was lonely without a partner in life. He was everything I wanted in a husband. His faith seemed strong, he was athletic, but what about children? We decided we could adopt. He was from a farm family with a full house. His mom and dad were the salt of the earth. He seemed very happy and I was too. My mom and dad also approved of our relationship. Marriage seemed more and more like a possibility as time passed.

We decided to go to the priest and talk to him about marriage. We found because he and I had both been divorced, we needed to get our first marriage annulled. Next, we filled out the papers and waited for the church to decide our future. After interviews were finished, both marriages were annulled. For both of us, it was obvious we were too young and did not truly understand the commitment of marriage and had rushed into our first relationships. Again, think about the times. Now at almost twenty-seven, I felt a little more settled in my journey. Our next hurdle was his diagnosis of mental illness. As mentioned before, he had been diagnosed as a manic/depressive. Today it is referred to as bi-polar. If you knew him and did not know the diagnosis, you would not have suspected it. He seemed fun-loving, jovial, loving, and full of life. He took medicine daily and had his condition under control. The priest would not marry us until he was convinced that we were ready. After many one-on-one interviews, the priest decided we were ready for this union. I loved Ron and knew we would have a wonderful life together. We started to focus on wedding plans. Since it was our second wedding, we decided to not wear the normal wedding attire. I chose an old-timey pink-lacey dress, and he wore a burgundy tux. Mike and Mary were our best man and matron of honor. The church was full, and it was a wonderful day. We had a reception that followed, and we went to Branson for our honeymoon. We had a great time and I was looking forward to the coming chapters of our life together. It seemed to be a perfect match. He fit right into the church family and everyone that met him liked him. He was funny, smart, and sweet.

CHAPTER EIGHT
~Another Mountain to Climb~

He was offered a full-time job at my school. He became a permanent substitute teacher and bus driver. We took students on fieldtrips and enjoyed new experiences with them. With our jobs at school we were able to buy a home in town which would cut way back on our gas expenses. We loved working with the high school kids. We even had a Bible study and a gathering of friends at our house. We usually had burgers and talked about life. We became involved with Teens Encounter Christ. TEC became very important to us. We became speakers and loved what we were doing. Many of our core group were involved with TEC as well. We were supported by our friends and life was good. When we weren't working with TEC, we were spending time with other Christian couples. We seemed to have a wonderful future ahead. I began again to think about a family. Adoption was a possibility. I was also willing to foster and then perhaps adopt. I was open to all the different options available. My husband was offered another job that would be more money and he could use his engineering skills.

His new job seemed to be a great fit. Our life together seemed almost perfect. Then one day, out of the blue, my husband disappeared. Were there missed signs or was I just naïve? Worried sick, I didn't have a clue where he was. I called everyone I knew, and no one had seen him or heard anything from him. After two days he called and told me he was in a hotel in a nearby town and wanted to come home. He seemed very troubled. I told him to come home and we would talk things out. We talked and talked about what had happened. I still felt uneasy, but he convinced me he was going to be OK. We had a TEC weekend coming up and he assured me this would never happen again. We went to the weekend and it was great. We were not speakers on the weekend, but we went to the gathering on Sunday. We were taking care of Mike's and Mary's daughter. We had a wonderful time with our friends and the kids on the TEC. I knew in my heart that the fear I felt when he disappeared was behind me. We went home after the weekend joyous and ready for the work week ahead. We had recently celebrated our first anniversary.

We had been married almost a year and one week. Other than the one disappearance, things seemed good. The Monday after the TEC weekend, he headed off to work as usual. We had a goodbye kiss and he waved as he climbed into his green Chevy truck. The day went pretty much as usual. I was still on summer vacation and did a little cleaning and prepared dinner. Cooking was a hobby that I enjoyed when school was out. This gave me time to prepare a homecooked meal. It was just about done. He would be home about 6:00 P.M. As time went by, I covered the food hoping it would keep warm or easily be heated up. Soon it was 7:00 P.M. and no word. I began to get worried. What could've happened to him? No cell phones or even beepers were being used yet. After another hour, I decided to try to call someone. The phone continued ringing at Ron's office and there was no answer. So, I called his boss's home number. He answered, and I asked if something had happened at work that would have made Ron this late? He said something had slowed down the project he was on and he had decided to go help on another job. He said he would call the other project manager and ask if Ron had made it and what time he had left. I thanked him and hung up. A few minutes later he called back and said that my husband had not made it to the second job site. What? That meant that no one had seen him since noon.

I called my friends, Mike and Mary, and told them the situation and they decided they would come over to keep me company. When they arrived, we tried not to talk about where my husband might be. We continued to talk about everything but the possibilities. We tried to focus on the TEC weekend. After a while it was time for bed, so they asked if I would be okay. "Yes," I was sure he had gone to a hotel somewhere to think. They gathered their daughter's clothes and toys and headed home.

Sleep eluded me. Staring at the ceiling, I waited for the phone to ring. Nothing. I tried to keep myself busy. The next morning it had been 24 hours. I decided to call my husband in as a missing person. The police said they could not classify him as missing until after 48 hours. At that point, they would actively begin a search. The minutes seemed like hours. The highway patrol had been contacted as well. The hospitals were contacted to see if any of them had an accident victim. There was no sign of him. His truck had not been spotted. It was like he had disappeared into thin air. By this time, I had gone to stay at my friends' home. Other friends continued to drop by to check on me. Still nothing was discovered of his where-abouts.

My mother's side of the family was having our family reunion and I decided to attend to get my mind off things. I prayed and tried to turn the worry over to God. Everyone asked where Ron was, and I just told them he could not make it. I did not go into any details. After visiting an hour or so, a policeman arrived at the door. He told me that I needed to go back to Rolla. A few breaks in the case had been discovered. I returned. No other information had been given. The drive was about 45 minutes, but it seemed more like 10 hours. I did not think I would ever make it to Mike and Mary's house. Upon arrival, everyone seemed on edge. No one was really talking about what was going on.

It had been a week and he had not been found. Now, finally, we had something that might help us find him. I was in the back of the house and someone else arrived. I could hear muffled voices from the living room and kitchen. As I went back to the front of the house, the vibe in the room had changed. Something had happened. Everyone became extremely quiet. Then someone started a conversation about the weather. It was a nice day but, there was a heaviness in the air. Something was wrong. I had a sick feeling in my stomach and began to feel like I could not breathe. My heart began to race. In a few minutes I was told by my wonderful friends that a report on the radio had stated that a body and a truck fitting the make, model, and color of my husband's truck had been found about 15 miles from Rolla. Maybe it was a mistake. How could this be reported on the radio without me being contacted first? I still had hope.

It was not too long before our friend, who was a highway patrolman, pulled into the driveway. My heart sank. I was speechless and I could not catch my breath. Watching him walk to the front door, he turned the doorknob and stepped into the room. His face was all telling. I knew it was not good news. Maybe it was not all bad. Ron's truck had been found. He looked straight at me. He had something very difficult to tell me. Tears filled his eyes and he said the authorities had found a body of a man that matched my husband's description. He went on to say that the police needed me to make a positive I.D. I could not comprehend his words. I thought I was going to suffocate or collapse. My heart was pounding in my ears. What? Identify? This meant the patrolmen knew it was Ron and needed me to verify it was indeed him. Wait, how could this be? My knees became weak. Someone took me by the arm and put me in a chair. My friend Mike stepped forward and asked if he could go instead of me. The patrolman nodded his head, yes. I could only imagine what Ron's body would look like. It had been a week since he disappeared.

I glanced over at him and knew in my heart that the patrolman and Mike were trying to protect me. I would have had a hard time unseeing what I had to see. After a quick hug, Mike and the patrolman left. I watched as they walked out to the patrol car. My husband had no family living in the immediate area. I knew the next week or so was going to be the most difficult time in my life to date.

It seemed like an eternity before they came back. As we all knew in our hearts, it was Ron. Mike did not relay any of the experience. He was very quiet when he returned. I knew by the look on his face that he had saved me from seeing the indescribable. They had found my husband in a cave on the side of a sinkhole. We had taken a group of students to the sinkhole on a fieldtrip when we were studying geography and geology of Missouri. Numb, I began to start to think about the funeral. Also, I had to call Ron's family and tell them he had been found. I don't really recall the conversation. It was like an out-of-body experience. The words were coming out of my mouth, but I was detached from the scene. I found out that his bloated body was found in rural Phelps county. He was found because a helicopter had spotted his green Chevrolet pickup parked under a tree. This was the first sighting that had seemed out of the ordinary. His body had been discovered by two young men hiking through the woods. Soon all policemen and highway patrolmen in the area swarmed to the scene to help control traffic on the small country road and retrieve the body. His body was in a state of deterioration. He had been shot in the head and a rifle was found beside him. The official report said he had committed suicide. What happened? The medicine had been working fine. What could have possibly brought this on?

We decided early on that his casket would remain closed. I began to ask myself and God what I had done to cause this to happen. I needed to know what went on the last few hours of his life. I talked to his boss and he gave me what information he had available. My husband had been on the job and something had caused a delay, so he decided to leave the job site and go to another. On his way to the other job site, he went by Wal-Mart and bought a rifle using our credit card. He then drove to the sinkhole and walked to the spot he had chosen to take his life. It was believed that he was not there very long until he pulled the trigger. What was he thinking the last minute of his life? Now, I wanted an answer to why? What brought this on? We will never really know. I kept telling myself that God was in control of my life. How could this tragedy be anything other than a tragedy?

An autopsy was performed, and it was believed he was not taking his medicine. Why? Some felt he had thought he had been cured and could manage on his own with the help of God and his church family. Everyone tried to assure me that I had done nothing to bring about his death. I still could not help but blame myself. I went back through every thought

and every word that I had spoken. My principal soon called
and told me I could take as much time as I needed before re-
turning to work. I decided I needed to go on. I had a purpose.
I just did not understand why this had happened. Many
prayers were said for me, and many prayers were said by me
to help me understand.

CHAPTER NINE
~Healing Hurts~

When school started, most of the kids were very supportive and wanted to help. But being from a small community, many rumors started to raise their ugly heads. Someone must have been cheating. The someone was probably me. It was not! As a matter of fact, cheating had not even entered my mind. Nor his for that matter. Even when I knew my first husband was cheating, I could never bring myself to cheat. Everyone kept asking why? Me included. Then I began to wonder what happened to my dream of a family? Now 27 years old and by myself again, time was running out. How could I possibly find someone and build a life with the family of my dreams? It seemed impossible. I learned somehow to live with judgmental stares and looks of disbelief from people who knew me personally and those that just knew who I was.

After about six months I tried to start going out some. Sitting at home and mourning was not in my best interest. When I decided to get out of the house, I found that most of my married friends were involved in varied couple activities at church. I again needed my church family and friends. Slowly but surely, things started to look a little brighter. Certainly, I was not ready to jump into any relationship. However, everyone felt they knew the perfect person for me, from fellow teachers to kids to friends. I went out to check the waters. None of them were of interest. It did, however, keep me busy and my mind off the lingering questions.

One of my cheerleaders, Yvonne, was having a problem with transportation because she lived twenty miles outside of town. Games, practices, and events became difficult for her.

She had talked to me a lot and had told me her mother and she were having problems. She asked if she could come stay with me until the end of the school year. It was about three months. I told her that her parents must agree and that I could act as her guardian until her graduation. She was 17. We came to a decision and she moved in.

In my heart, I was helping her. But in the end, she was helping me. The girl loved housework and kept my house spotless. After about two or three weeks she thought she had the perfect person for me. I tried but still no connection. She continued to try as did others, but nothing was happening to help me find the family I so wanted. I had decided a long time ago that I would adopt if I had to. Maybe I would have to raise adopted babies by myself. Each night I asked for a sign that my life would somehow turn itself around and get what I thought was back on track. It seemed forever before I had a dream that opened my heart to possibilities. Then again, how could a dream really foretell anything?

One evening I was trying to clear my mind and watch a little television to escape for a while. After a nice quiet evening of sitcoms, I decided to turn in. I went to sleep easily, which was a change. In a dream Ron appeared to me. It was a wedding. At first, all I saw was my deceased husband. His straight blonde hair made him easy to identify. He was in the burgundy tux he had worn during our wedding. Soon I appeared at his side in the pink dress I had worn. He told me it was time to move on. He took my left hand and a tall black-haired man with a beard walked up behind him. His hair was much like Tony Orlando's from back in the day. It was shoulder length. My deceased husband gently placed my hand in the new man's hand and faded into the background. I could not see the face of this tall stranger. Then I awoke with a start. What had just happened? Was it a sign? Or just a weird dream. I could not help but feel it was something very special. Praying for my head to clear, sleep again came over me.

I shared the dream with a few of my friends and began immediately to think of every black-haired man I knew. He was not anyone I knew because the only men that met this description were much younger than me and the hair and beard did not fit. I felt like I needed to go out and look for someone to fit the description. I know now I did not need to find him. He needed to find me. So, I tried to clear my mind and continue my life working with kids and keeping my options open.

One evening, I was rushing out my front door when an aqua colored Gremlin came up the hill. A Gremlin was an American Motors Corporation made compact car back in the 1970s. I saw three small heads in the car seats, and I glanced up at the driver. For some reason our eyes locked for a second and then I noticed his black hair and beard. He made a right turn and continued back down to a house on the side of the hill. I shook it off and continued to my car, got in, started the engine and headed to school for a game. I don't think I had ever seen this man before and I did not recognize the car.

Time marched on and I tried to keep my mind occupied with the kids at school and participating in church activities. I even continued working on TEC teams. I would work be-hind the scenes. I really tried to be positive and I continued praying and made an honest effort to learn more about myself and my spiritual life. Many nights I would go to sleep listen-ing to taped sermons from some of my favorite preachers. I tried to watch spiritual shows on TV and surround myself with spiritual people. There were times when I felt very lost and alone. But through prayer and a little help from my friends, I would snap back. Being surrounded by loving friends and my students gave me a reason to get up each morning. There were several couples that I hung out with; Mike and Mary, Dick and Pat, Tom and Kathy, Bruce and Dottie, and P. J. and Linda were only a few. They were all happily married and raising their children. I so wanted what they had. Was it not meant to be? I just did not understand.

Approaching my 28th birthday, I had just about given up. One thing I noticed was that I had never really allowed myself forgiveness for what had happened to Ron. One night I decided to write my prayer down so I could not only feel my prayer but see it. I have moved many times since that night, so the actual paper is most likely in a box somewhere. It will, however, forever be etched in my mind and heart.

"Dear God, thank you for helping me through the hard times I have experienced the last five years. I could have never made it without you and my friends. Thank you for bringing Mike and Mary to me. They are more than a brother and sister to me. They are part of me and who I am because I don't know if I could have made it without them. Mike stepped up and identified Ron for me. I can never thank him enough for that. Honestly, I don't know how. Mike and Mary have stood with me through this year of unbelievable loss. Feelings of fault just would not go away.

"I am so confused. I felt I have known my purpose for such a long time. The kids at school are terrific and I help them as much as I can. Also, my support for them is very important to me. Young people had an important part of my heart. I still don't have the one thing I have desired since I

40

was very young, a family. I don't understand. My 28th birthday is coming soon, and I feel my time is running out. Why God? If I am misunderstanding what I am supposed to do, then somehow show me the way. Show me my purpose. Could my big family I always wanted simply be my students? I am ready to step out and move on. My heart has a hole in it. I still hope there is someone for me. Was the dream just a weird thing or did it mean something? If I am going down the wrong path, show me the way. Mike and Mary are supporting me in every way possible. Other friends have also stepped up to help. They even intercepted my bill for the gun and paid it, so I would not have to come face to face with the weapon that Ron had used.

"Again, I thank you for my church family and friends. Their support is more than I could have ever expected. Please help me find what I am supposed to do. If there is someone, I am ready. I will be strong. Continue to grant me your grace and let your peace flow over me. Amen"

At the end of writing this prayer I felt a calming. Peace and joy seemed to fill the void I had felt so long. The following day I went to school with a lighter heart. As soon as I walked in, I came face to face with my principal. He informed me that we were going to make up a snowed-out game that night. Really?! Looking forward to the night off, this was not a welcomed development. Dang, I did not want to go to that game. But, as God planned it, I had no choice. I tried to convince myself it would be OK, but I was not listening. The day had started so well, now this! After school I ran home to grab something to eat. I was really getting tired of concession stand food. I changed into a school T-shirt and jeans and headed back to the gym. I was not a joyous servant.

I parked my car, gathered up the stuff I needed and headed into the gym. There were not many people there so far, so I found a spot in the bleachers and planted myself. I began talking to some of my cheerleaders. It was getting close to game time and most of the girls ran out for their last potty break for a while. Julie, one of the girls, stayed sitting next to me. She had already made the trip. As we chatted, the gym began to fill up because game time was near. I scanned the crowd and I looked toward the concession stand. A man appeared in the doorway. He was a big guy. He was about 6 foot 5 inches. He had long black hair and a full black beard. He was Tony Orlando, Tom Selleck, and Sam Elliot all rolled into one. In his arms was a small boy. The child was around two years old. The man held the hand of another small boy, around six years of age, This towering male seemed to be encircled by a light. Obviously, just the light from the concession stand. But it sure caught my attention and seemed to make him glow. I asked Julie who he was. She replied, "His name is Kent. He is my cousin. He is divorced and has custody of his boys. Do you want to go out with him?" I said "Maybe." About that time a third boy showed up. He was a little older, maybe seven. The foursome took their seats in the bleachers across the gym from where I was sitting. It so happened they were right in front of my Mom and Dad. They were also sitting by Julie's dad.

At half-time, I noticed Kent had headed to the concession stand. I am sure he wanted to get the boys popcorn to keep them busy while watching the game. He stood by the door entering the gym. His hands rested on the door frame above his head. He was obviously waiting for the concession line to die down. I decided to get a closer look. Kent also had a cousin playing on the team. So, he watched as the team was warming up. I made up a reason to go to the other side of the gym. As I went through the door, I looked up at him and with my sweetest voice said "Hi." He looked straight down at me and said absolutely nothing. Not even a smile. After the game was over, I watched as he left. He and the boys headed out the door and loaded into an aqua Gremlin. The very one that had come up the hill in front of my house. The very man I had locked eyes with before.

What I did not know at the time was that his uncle had pointed me out and told Kent he should ask me out. I also did not know that he was shy. Julie had my number and I told her to give it to him. When he didn't call, I chalked it up to not interested. Later I found out he thought I was speaking to someone else when I said hello. The reason he had not been able to watch his cousin Jeff play before was because it normally conflicted with his work schedule. This rescheduled game had made it possible for him to come see him play. After the game, his aunt told him I was interested in meeting him. His aunt gave him my phone number and he did not call so after a few days I called Selma (his aunt) and asked if he had seemed at all interested. She said he was uneasy about calling. He was afraid I would say no. He thought it was a joke. She thought I should call him. I had never done this before, but desperate times called for desperate measures. So, that evening I gave him a call. I had been playing volleyball at church one night a week. I decided to ask him to go play. He said yes. The courtship began!

Kent met many of my friends that night and seemed to fit in. Playing volleyball made it easier for him because he had always been very quiet and not comfortable around a bunch of people, especially those he didn't know. At one time I looked back at him to see if he looked like he was enjoying the volleyball game and his eyes were sparkling and he gave me a flirty little wink. The next chapter of my life had begun.

We started seeing each other almost every night. We would either meet at my house or I would go to his. The kids were always present, and a relationship began to develop with them. They along with their dad seemed like they were glad I was there. After about four months, the rental house next to mine was vacated. I checked into it and found it was within his budget. He rented it immediately and moved in within a couple weeks. I was helping him with the boys, and since the two older ones went to the same school that I taught, it made sense for them to come to my room after school. They went home with me and we picked up the youngest at the babysitter. When Kent got home, he came over and usually ate dinner. Then at bedtime they walked home. As time passed, I began to develop very strong feelings for Kent and the boys. My athletic background helped because I could play almost any outside game the boys wanted. We were having a great time and bonding. We went on picnics at the river and life was good.

I did not know that number two son, Jaimie, was a sleep-walker. One night after Kent and the boys went home, I stayed up a little while grading papers. I decided it was time to go to bed and I drifted off to sleep. Realize, in the eighties no one ever locked their doors at night in small town Missouri. In my sleep, I suddenly felt like someone was standing in my room staring at me. I was hesitant to open my eyes, but when I did, I had a small figure leaning over me eyes wide open but apparently sound asleep. It was Jaimie. I guided him

44

into the extra bedroom and put him in bed and covered him up. I locked the doors. I called Kent and told him he had a missing kid. The next morning, he came over and collected his son. He started locking his door. Jaimie had left his room, gone out the front door, walked across two yards and into my bedroom without waking up. The next morning, he did not remember a thing.

After about five months of spending about every evening together, we began to discuss the future. He hinted at marriage and said something like, "Maybe we should give it a try?" We found a pastor that was willing to marry us. I was considered a widow and he was divorced. It was not as easy to find someone as one might think. After we talked to a young preacher, he felt we should become a family. So, with our parents and the boys we were married. We made sure the boys were involved in the ceremony. Later, we hoped we could be married in the Catholic church. We had to go through the annulment process again for him. So, our little family was bonded together forever. We both felt very strongly about that. This was my third marriage and his second. Everything in the world was against us. Kent, Raimie (seven), Jaimie (six), Toby (two), and I were beginning a new life. I was more than excited about our future. My mother was very concerned that I may not be ready for this new life. The last five years had been very difficult on her too. A mom always wants to protect her children, no matter how old they are. I, however, had an amazing peace and confidence that I could do this. By this time, I knew this was all part of God's plan.

In my soul, I knew this was no longer my plan. For those who do not think God has a sense of humor, my prayer for a family was answered in a big way. This was not quite the way

I planned it, but God's plan had prepared me for this new life. I also knew I had to deal with Ron's suicide. On the surface I was doing fine. My head was ready to move on. Although deep in my heart, I knew I had to reach a greater understanding of what had happened and somehow realize it was not my fault. I had to understand that life is a process and along the way there will be pain. This pain we feel helps us grow in our spirit and faith. Also, I had to learn that I would not be the person I was, if my life plan had gone perfectly. What would have happened if I hadn't gone through the divorce and the suicide? Would I have been ready to help raise three little boys? I did not want to replace their mother, but I did want to be a mother to them. They deserved that. I had no real problem adjusting to cooking for five. The groceries were unreal including seven gallons of milk at a pop. I loved to cook. But laundry, going from one to five. Oh my gosh! I had no idea how many clothes three boys could go through. So, we left for school each morning with the washer running and came home in the evening and started another load.

Since I was getting close to twenty-nine, I felt our time was running out to adopt. We began to talk about adding to our family. We were hoping for a little girl. Twenty-eight and I had never conceived. So, chances were the doctors were correct. I could never conceive.

I was working at the Forest Service at the time. I was a crew leader for the YCC. This was a federal high school program that put teenagers to work during the summer. This was a great job for a teacher such as me. It was an outside job and I loved it. We cleaned up campgrounds, fixed fences, and cut brush. The summer was especially hot that year. One day I felt dizzy. I thought it was just the heat. So, I figured it would pass. It did not. I felt very disoriented. So, I took the next day off and went to the doctor. He did a complete physical and then the doctor asked if I could be pregnant. I replied, "I don't think so because I have not experienced any other symptoms." To be safe, he wanted to do a pregnancy test. We did, and I was! I was shocked but so excited. We were so excited. We did not want to tell anyone yet. It was a good call. Only a week or so had passed when I hemorrhaged. Kent took me to the hospital after we called someone to watch the kids. I lost the baby. Two days after the miscarriage, I started cramping again. The pain was intense. Kent helped me to the bathroom, and I was bleeding again. At first, I had no idea what was happening. Finally, I passed a part of the fetus left behind by the miscarriage. Again, why Lord? I thought it could be my age or some other complication I did not know I had. After another look, my doctor said it would be difficult for me to conceive and even harder to carry a baby full term. I felt that God would take care of it and if I was supposed to have a baby of my own, I would. After all I had a beautiful family. I still wanted to try and see what happened. A girl would be nice.

A few months later, I felt dizzy again. I also had other symptoms. Hunger, unbelievable hunger was always present. I was so blessed because somehow morning sickness had escaped me. What could this be? Maybe just maybe. It was. This time I felt wonderful. I did have a little dizziness, but all in all it was an easy pregnancy. My baby was due on my birthday, February 18th. On February 6th, I went in for my regular checkup and the doctor asked if I was taking afternoon naps. What? No one had told me to do that. I was still teaching. My room was on the second floor. Unfortunately, the restroom was on the first floor. My doctor told me to call my principal and tell him I would not be back until after my six-week maternity leave. That was on Wednesday and the same week on Friday at 6:00 AM I got up to go to the restroom. While I was in the restroom, my water broke. The baby was ten days early. Kent again was a trooper. He called the sitter, and we left within ten minutes. By this time, I knew I was in labor. The weather was bad. It was snowing and cold. When we arrived, they examined me and told us I was indeed having the baby. Already at three centimeters, my pains were getting closer and closer together. I had planned on a natural delivery. By 9:30 AM, the nurses came to check me one more time and found I was ready to go. There was one major problem, the baby had somehow flipped and was breech. At ten centimeters,the doctor decided a C-section was necessary. So, they gave me an epidural. I was numb from the waist down. They also put me under. I counted backwards for two seconds and I was gone. When I came to, I saw Kent first and he said we had our baby girl. This was before we could find out the sex during the pregnancy. The nurse and doctor came in and said she was perfect. I didn't have the words to express my joy. When I held her, I felt so full of love. She was so precious. We named her Brandie. What would the boys think? They were ten, eight and five. They immediately became her protectors. They seemed thrilled with their little sister.

This was all good until she became the little tagalong that was constantly bugging them. My sweet little girl became tough because she really felt she was the boss. So, she was a tomboy and loved sports. At three she became the cheer mascot and cheered with the girls. Also, at three in her swimming class, she without hesitation jumped off the high dive. No fear. She learned to play basketball at a young age and was very competitive. She seemed to be very confident and loved to be involved in most sports. She fit right in. Both Kent and I had been very active playing softball on the church league and Kent played college basketball and basketball in the Airforce. After going through several sports most of the kids settled on basketball. In high school, Toby decided to play tennis as well. Our little family was very happy. I am not saying there wasn't sibling rivalry, especially the two older boys. Since they were so competitive, they could argue about almost anything. But the other side of this, we had four kids that totally defended each other. As time passed the boys became better and better at basketball. So perhaps a college scholarship was a real possibility. We focused on good grades and Kent worked with the kids and even coached their basketball teams. He also became a Scoutmaster. For a year or so every time we went camping, we had eight extra boys or so in addition to our four kids. I was always involved too. Inevitably, we were a very busy family.

It seemed I was getting very tired by the end of the day. Energy seemed to evade me. At night it seemed I would finally go to sleep after making many mental notes of what I needed to do the next day. I was still coaching and going to a couple of games a week. Church was on Sundays and sometimes more. Grading papers and lesson plans filled any spare time I had. With our other activities on top of that and the mountains of *laundry*, we were always on the move. Now we had a little girl in the mix.

CHAPTER TEN - WHAT?
~HERE WE GO AGAIN~

When Brandie was about 3 ½ years old, I began to get a little dizzy again. What was going on? I also was starving all the time. I thought about pregnancy, but the doctor had said it would be almost impossible. He said I had been extremely lucky before. I was a bit concerned and decided to go to the doctor to see what in the world was wrong with me. After checking me out, the doctor said we should do a pregnancy test just in case. It turned out to be positive. Yes, I was pregnant again! I let myself adjust to this news and thought how great is this? We had to prepare for a fifth child. What would we do? Our house was very small for a family of six. We needed to make some adjustments. We may have to put the three older boys in the basement and the two younger kids upstairs in the second bedroom. This would work for a while. Then we would have to move to another house. The basement had paneling, and we purchased some rugs. We managed to get two water beds for the two older boys and a new mattress for Toby for his bed under the stairs. At least they had their own bed and little space. We divided the room with a bookshelf. This would have to do until we could figure things out when the family was indeed larger and older.

The pregnancy was not as easy as my second one. I did not have morning sickness, but the hunger was ever present. It seemed the weight piled on twice as fast as before. By the time I was five months, I looked like I was eight months. I really was trying to watch what I ate. The doctor decided to do some tests. Something was not right. My blood pressure skyrocketed. This never had been a problem before, and I lost the baby weight quickly after birth. The tests gave us some answers. We found I had pre-eclampsia, which is a potentially dangerous pregnancy complication characterized by high blood pressure, swelling of the feet and hands, and protein in the urine. This would make this pregnancy so much more difficult. The due date was set for the middle of October. At least the last two months would not be in the heat of summer. Of course, teaching was a good job for me, because I was off all summer. I could rest in the afternoons and keep track of my blood pressure. I did have four kids at home. For the most part, they were old enough to help. Brandie was four, so she did not quite understand what was happening. I thank goodness for the older boys. As time went on, the pounds seemed to multiply. The first week in September, my doctor put me in the hospital. The doctor knew another C-section was going to be necessary. The only problem was our local hospital did not want to do the surgery. They were afraid they would lose our baby and me. They had lost a mother and her baby just a week earlier. I tried to calm myself because my blood pressure was 215/114. While waiting for a decision, I was bedfast and could only have a visitor once a day for 10 minutes. Kent got to see me, but I couldn't even watch television. I could listen to easy listening music. Finally, the doctors decided to transport me with a helicopter to St. Louis. They felt Barnes Hospital would be the best place for me and our child. As an afterthought, the doctors felt the helicopter would cause even more stress. They decided to send me by ambulance. They would call my husband and fill him in. He was at work and we had three kids in school and one at the babysitter. Our cousin had promised he would be on call and his mom was two houses away to assist. They were contacted and agreed to stay with the kids indefinitely. It was good to have family so nearby.

I was sedated and loaded into the ambulance. I prayed that God would take care of our baby and me. Kent followed the ambulance and had a hard time keeping up. He said it was running about 90 miles an hour. It felt like it was the fastest trip to St. Louis ever. Upon arrival the paramedics rushed me into the ER. They immediately started running tests. When Kent arrived, he found that I was stable, but the doctors said they were going to run a few more tests to see if the baby was in danger. Kent decided to run back home to get everything organized, so he could just come and stay if need be. He went to work to organize what people could do if he was gone for an extended time. At 2:30 PM the next day the hospital called Kent and he was told the doctors would be doing an emergency C-section at 4:00 PM. He had an hour and a half to make a two-hour drive. He made it just in time to put on the mask and gown and be led into the operating room. This was the guy who tended to faint in hospitals. All six feet five inches of him, flat on the floor. He thought he was just saying good-bye and giving me a kiss before I was taken into surgery. Instead he walked directly into the operating room, just as they cut me open. Much to his surprise they let him stay. I was sedated and not totally under, so I was glad he was there and on his feet. I could feel them cutting the incision from hipbone to hipbone.

I told Kent the pain was almost unbearable. I didn't know if I could stand it. The doctor assured me I was only imagining. No, I was not. As they started pulling the baby, I told them I could not handle the pain. They did a few pokes with a pin to see if I could feel anything. Yes, I could. They decided to give me more anesthesia. After a few minutes they tried again. The pain was gone but they told me I would still feel pressure. I did. There was no pain like before. Kent was telling me step by step what was going on. The baby was finally out. The nurse took the baby to clean him up and asked Kent if he wanted to help. As he went to help, he saw our son for the first time. He was so tiny, 4 pounds 5 ounces. They told Kent and me that my tubes should be tied because having another baby would be deadly for me and a baby. The tubes were tied. I was 34 and raising five children. Our family was complete. Dustin was perfect in every way, just tiny. I had to stay in the hospital for a week because he had to reach at least five pounds. Kent could literally hold him in his hand. His head rested on Kent's fingers, his bottom on the palm of his hand, and his feet dangled down his arm. He was soooooo tiny. Granny had knitted him a sweater and cap set that swallowed him, so she went to work and made him a new one preemie size. I would have never thought that he would grow into a 6 foot 4 inch young man and basketball player. At his four-week checkup he was six pounds twelve ounces. He was totally healthy. I had found out later that the doctors did not know if either of us would make it. God indeed looked after us.

One week after the birth we were on our way home. As we put him in the car seat, we had to laugh. He was so incredibly small. The kids were anxious to meet their little brother. They were *very* excited. They at first were afraid to hold him. I too was somewhat scared. Hurting him was a real concern to me. Finally, the doctor and nurses convinced me he was just like any other baby. He continued growing very quickly and caught up with other babies his age. Now here I am. My prayers have been answered in a big way. My big family was complete. I began to focus on my life and becoming the best wife, mom, daughter, daughter-in-law, granddaughter-in-law, coach and teacher that I could. My life was indeed busy.

CHAPTER ELEVEN
~Back to School~

When Dustin was five months old, my husband convinced me to go back to school and get my Master's degree. He was very supportive, so I went one night a week to school. The advanced degree also paid off economically. It absolutely helped get jobs when Kent had to move because of his work. Each time we had to relocate someone had approached him with a better offer. His offer from a city close by to become its city manager, called for a change. The kids would attend a new school. They were not happy about moving. They had their friends and their sports. Anyone who knows about sports, moving means starting all over. You must earn your spot on the new teams. They no longer were automatically the starters on their teams. They had to work hard to achieve that position.

As a family of seven, my life seemed to be consumed with busyness. I am helping raise five children. All the while I am still teaching, coaching, helping our parents when needed and being a student myself. My organization became very important. I had little or no time for myself. Cooking became a major event and going out to eat was non-existent. We could cook as quick as going out because it was seven miles to the nearest restaurant. As the boys got older, it was like cooking for a small army. We went through so much food and milk. Crockpot meals, banquet chicken and frozen meat dishes became staples. Shake-and-bake was also a quick meal. We baked a lot of potatoes. The first meal the kids prepared was usually shake-and-bake porkchops or porksteaks, baked potatoes, and a vegetable. All have become great cooks.

They also learned to do laundry. This came about because I started to notice clean folded clothes in the dirty clothes basket. It was easier to put clean clothes in the dirty clothes basket than to put them away. I wish I had thought of that as a kid, but I usually helped mom on Saturday do all the laundry. We hung up all the clothes. They were on the clothesline outside or on the clothesline dad built in the basement. In the future, the kids would know how to take care of themselves in college. Also, their future spouses would be happy.

As mentioned before, we had to move for Kent's new job. He had to have a local address as the city manager. Our youngest was eighteen months, our one and only girl was just five, and the older boys were ten, thirteen, and fifteen. We found a perfect house for us. It was an earth-sheltered home about half of a mile from the Meramec River. We also had five acres, a barn, and an out-building. We had camping and boating rights on the river. The older boys loved the camping, floating, and swimming. We had enough land to house a couple of horses. Brandie and I always loved horses. We were able to go for a ride periodically. We had to keep the horses fed and their stalls cleaned out, which was difficult sometimes.

One day Brandie and I were riding around our property and I was having problems with my saddle. I asked Kent to tighten it for me. He did and suddenly Rosebar (my horse) decided to start bucking. I was barely a horse rider and was NOT experienced enough to stay on a bucking horse. I managed to stay aboard for about three bucks. In my mind of minds, I thought I would just jump off. My mind and body had a disconnect and I went soaring about fifteen feet in the air (this was not part of my perfect life I had pictured). I landed on my tailbone knocking the air out of me. Kent did

56

not know whether to run after the horse or help me. He made the right choice. As soon as I got my wind back, he helped me up. God was watching because it was a miracle I had not been hurt. Everything seemed like it was working. My pride was hurt, and I had an unbelievable bruise but I seemed fine. At the time it was not funny. Now I can think about it and laugh. Kent said it was quite a funny sight.

The kids adapted to the new school quite well. They made friends and things were looking good. It was about this time that our oldest became a handful. Sibling rivalry raised its ugly head and we were off and running. The two oldest boys were very competitive. They would get into physical fights that I could not stop. Now they were as tall as me and physically, I could not break them apart. My prayers were many. After all, I had been a great kid or at least I thought so. I had no siblings close to my age to fight, so I did not have any experience in such things. I had to figure out how to handle this without getting totally upset myself.

My friend Mike came to the rescue. He had been raised in a blended family. He gave me his stepmom Colleen's phone number and told me to call her when I was at the end of my rope. It worked. She talked me through many confrontations. How could these sweet little boys have turned into these unruly fighting teenagers? It was kind of funny in a way because I began to realize they never hit each other in the face. They always hit each other in the chest, for vanity's sake? We obviously made it through those years and our kids are still alive and well. I think God looks out for kids unless he has another plan. Sometimes I wonder how I lived through my childhood. I even remember jumping out of haylofts on to stacks of hay on the ground. I climbed trees as well as any boy and never had a broken bone until I was in my fifties.

After about seven years of marriage to Kent, I realized that I had not really understood and accepted my ex-husband's suicide. One night, while on vacation in Texas, sleep was totally eluding me. Everyone else was sound asleep. I slipped out into the living-room. Shutting the bedroom door behind me, I settled on the couch and turned on the TV adjusting the volume, so I would not wake anyone. I turned to the CMT channel and began listening to the music. A song came on that I had listened to many times but never really listened closely to the words. These words changed my whole view of my ex-husband's suicide. The song was "The Dance" sung by Garth Brooks and written by Tony Arata.

"Looking Back on the Memories" invited me to reminisce about the year Ron and I had spent as husband and wife. For a moment, the world seemed right. "How could I have known you would ever say goodbye?" These words caught my soul off-guard. I did not know. Should I still be blaming myself? I did not understand his state of mind. The weekend had been great before he vanished.

As I sat in the silence another set of words grabbed my heart as never before. I could have missed the pain, but I would have missed the dance. The dance is the life we share with others. Our relationships are what makes up this dance of our time on earth. The love, the sorrow, one's spiritual walk all a part of the choreography of life. We choose our individual steps. These steps hopefully lead us toward God's purpose. The wrong move can sometimes change our lives in a moment. Listening to God's voice does not always mean it will be what one wants to hear. If we continue in prayer someday the wisdom will come.

58

Our life is better left to chance. As a believer, I hope that I will be able to discern what God has shown me. Through life's experiences we gain wisdom which helps us choose joy over sorrow in many if not all of life's challenges. Through joy we can be kind and understanding to others no matter the situation. Would anyone like to know exactly how life will go? God is in control and if followers are capable of listening, life would be so much simpler.

God indeed works in mysterious ways! I wrote a letter to Garth telling him how much his song meant to me and how it allowed me to live free from guilt. I was fortunate enough to get to express to him personally about the song and the way it had touched me. I also began to see my life wasn't left to chance but was God's plan. I had for a long time thought the plan I had was all mine. I just had to get out of the way. The words had spoken to my heart like I had never heard them before. I had survived nine rough years, but I began to see this period of my life completely different. I had loved during those difficult years and was blessed by friends, etc. Hopefully, I was a blessing to other people in my life as they had been in mine. If these times had been only according to my plan, my life would have turned out much differently. These events led to personal growth and a better understanding of my purpose.

I knew absolutely that I would never have wanted to miss my marriage to Ron. I loved him. Our year together was beautiful. He had opened my eyes to adopting because he had been told he could not father a child. In the past, I too was told it would be hard for me to conceive. My heart was opened to raising children other than my own. Little did I know that this change of heart helped me accept what I thought was the inevitable. But God had his plan, not only was I chosen to raise our three boys, he gave us two more children that I wasn't supposed to have.

In the meantime, Kent's father, Leo, had been diagnosed with Alzheimer's. We were trying to help his folks as much as possible. Leo passed away five years after being diagnosed. Shortly after Kent's dad passed, his mom, Dee, had a major stroke. Dee was the caregiver for his dad as well as her mom, Granny. Dee and Granny could no longer live independently. His sister, Vicki, was a single parent raising her son, so we offered to bring his mother and grandmother to live with us.

My mom was now living alone. My dad had died when Brandie was only eighteen months old and my mother was sixty-two. My mom was doing well and remarried at age seventy. She married a widower that she had known for the biggest part of her life.

We moved Granny and Dee in with our family of seven. I was still teaching and coaching. Kent of course was working, so we found a young woman from church that would watch them during the day and, as soon as I arrived home from school, I was on duty. The kids helped, and we did fine for a while.

One child in diapers, three in sports, and a five-year-old princess was challenge enough, but somehow God gave me enough energy to continue teaching and coaching. I also was a wife, a daughter, a daughter-in-law and a granddaughter-in-law. I won't lie. Some days were very difficult. People told me periodically they did not know how I did it. My faith was all I had. It was the only thing that kept me going. With God's help I managed to take care of everyone, even me, a little bit.Our house was full of love and challenges, but I wouldn't change any part of that special time living with four generations of our family

CHAPTER TWELVE
~GRASS IS GREENER~

Rai, number one son, again was experiencing adjusting to young adulthood and needed a break. He was sixteen and felt his parents did not have a clue about life. He became somewhat rebellious. He started making a lot of long-distance phone calls to New Jersey to his biological mom and others he had met during visits. Of course, everything was greener on the other side of the fence. At the end of his sophomore year, he wanted to move to New Jersey. After he had run our phone bill up $1000.00, we said fine. He was told he could not just jump back and forth. He would have to stay a whole year. He learned everyone had rules and he needed to follow them. After a year, he came back home. He had given up his starting position on the varsity basketball team, so he usually was the sixth man in. He finished high school and after high school, he had several jobs and wasn't happy in any of them. He was lost as what to do, so he decided to join the army giving himself time to grow up. We hoped this would help him find direction and in turn make a better decision about his future. The army did its job. It made a man out of him. He got out a little early and went to college. He used the G.I. Bill and played basketball. He met his wife while finishing his degree and returned to the army as an officer. He spent a lot of time overseas and we really missed being with him and his family. He recently retired after twenty years of service. These decisions allowed him the time needed. He is presently working for the government and he and his wife of 23 years have three girls and one boy. Shannon has a degree in psychology but for now is a stay-at-home mom taking care of their busy household.

Jaimie, number two son, was still a freshman in high school and going through self- awareness issues. He sometimes felt insecure about his abilities and was searching for who he was. The year that Rai was away was a good thing for Jaimie because he came into his own. He proved to be an excellent basketball player and was not in the shadow of Rai. Jaimie hit a long half-court shot at the end of a homecoming game and won it. The crowd went wild and he became somewhat of a hero. He became more personally aware after this and he began to grow as a person. Rai came back his senior year, they played together for a year. Jaimie's senior year, he was named the most valuable player. He too continued playing in college. He came back home with just a few hours left to finish his degree. He met his wife that summer. She was a hometown girl and was committed to join the Air Force. Jaimie ended up joining the Army. He was destined for something great just like Rai. After his four years in the Army, he had a few different jobs, but none was really suited for him. Jennifer, Jaimie's wife, left the Air Force early and she and Jaimie married and had two children while in the service. They have been married twenty-three years. Again, we did not get to see as much of them as we would have liked. After they came back home, he got a job at the bus plant. By this time, he knew he needed to finish his degree. Jaimie and Jen began to attend a Methodist church in Claremore. This was the same church that Jen had attended during her childhood. They became very involved and Jaimie began to blossom. Sometimes it takes a transformation of heart to get on board with God's plan. Jaimie was searching for his purpose. He had trained as a lay speaker and sometimes spoke when he was needed. God dropped Jaimie's purpose right in his lap.

The church needed a new Youth Director. Jaimie had some very special gifts. He was a very good energetic speaker. When he told me he had applied for the job, I knew he was going to get it. Another prayer answered. He spent several years at this job. The youth program grew, and he touched many young hearts. In the meantime, Kent and I had started attending church there also. As Jaimie grew in his faith, the Pastor saw he would be a great candidate for the ministry. Jaimie finished his degree. A decision was made to pursue his call to ministry. He is now an associate pastor and has his own congregation, Vessel. When the south campus (Vessel) started, it was quite small, but the word-of-mouth spread quickly. The church grew rapidly. He is now finishing up seminary and Jaimie is very happy. His wife, son and daughter are flourishing. Jaimie's and Jennifer's kids are now in Belize on a mission trip. Jennifer works as a sales manager for a speciality metal distributor. Our two oldest had found their niche. Three more to go.

Toby, number three son, was in fifth grade when we moved to Cuba, Missouri. He was the shyest of the older boys. He had a great sense of humor and developed a few close friends. He played basketball in junior high but turned to tennis in high school. We moved to near Tulsa, Oklahoma his senior year. This was a difficult move for him. At seventeen, starting a new school, proved a major challenge for our shy son. After graduation he decided to go to New Jersey for a while. He got a job and stayed about a year. He came back home and had a few jobs locally and had thoughts of entering the military too. This did not work out, so he began to look for something that paid well. Remember, he was the child that could fix anything. He could also build things like furniture or even buildings. He began to work at a local restaurant as their handyman. Here he met his future wife. He was very talented and ended up going into carpentry, became a journeyman, and worked his way up the ladder. After he married Robyn, he began working for his father-in-law and travelled. We did not see them as much as we would have liked but that is what happened with all the kids at one time or another. They had two boys and as they approached school age, they wanted the boys to attend the school at which I was teaching and coaching. Robyn had also attended this same school through ninth grade. Verdigris was and is known as a great school. By this time, Brandie and Dustin were in college. My mom was now living with us. She moved in at 77 years old after the loss of my stepdad. Mom was still healthy and could take care of herself. I would check on her at lunch and made a point to get home as quickly as I could after practice. We managed to keep her at home for another ten years. At 87 we had to take her to a nursing home. One day after a short trip to Walmart, we came home and found mom getting ready to throw water from a pitcher on the fire in the fireplace. She did not remember it was a gas fireplace. We could not leave her alone even for a few minutes. She was in the same facility as Dee, Kent's mom.

Toby's family came to live with us while he was travelling. Kent was now working on the road also. He was in Wyoming working on a pipeline as an engineer/inspector. Toby finally made his way back home and is now a supervisor and works with a company that remodels hospitals to make them more efficient. Robyn works in the administrative office at school. They have been married twenty-two years.

At this point we were very proud of the three older boys.

The younger two kids seemed to be adapting fine to the new school and house. During all these times of transition, we knew we had to pray for two more to find their perfect career. Brandie was going to be in junior high and Dustin was going into second grade when we moved to Verdigris.

Brandie, our baby girl, was the outgoing very confident one of the kids (she disagrees)! She was an athlete and a musician. All the older kids had been in band, but she was the most naturally talented. She immediately became a starter on the basketball team and a member of the jazz band which was a tryout only band. She made a lot of friends quickly. She also played soccer and was on the track team. She was in the homecoming court multiple times. Between her freshman and sophomore year we went to New York for modelling. She was offered a chance to go to Milan the following summer. After the summer in New York, she decided she wanted to be a kid a little longer. With good grades and talent, she too was heading for a great future. Her senior year she was a basketball All-Stater, an academic All-Stater and a two-time state runner-up in high jump and two-time state high jump champion. She was offered scholarships in both track and basketball. She decided on basketball. She wanted to go into the medical field and majored in biology and chemistry. After graduation, she continued her education to become an RN. She worked at a major Tulsa hospital for ten years. While there she met her husband, Rusty, who was also an RN. He worked in the ER. She now works as a liaison between major hospitals in our region to an extended care facility. She helps families pick out the best facility for their needs. Rusty is working in a Dialysis Lab and administers dialysis to patients. They have been married eleven years and have one son, Ryder.

Dustin, number five child, was the easiest to raise because he was smart enough to watch the older kids and learn from their mistakes. He was shy, but very likeable, so he did develop friendships quickly. He made his friends mostly through sports. He started out with soccer, basketball, and t-ball. When he was older, he tried football, but because of an injury left it after his eighth grade year. Baseball wasn't his thing either, so he settled on basketball and soccer. Dustin was always busy and loved being outside. He spent hours on the trampoline. He too became a very good basketball player. His senior year he was named the MVP and was the Homecoming King. He went on to play basketball and soccer in college. He finished his degree in communications. After college he worked for a restaurant as a management candidate but decided he really did not want to work in the restaurant business his entire life. He stepped out and submitted his application to a major police department. There were about five-hundred applicants and only fifty were chosen. He was one of the fifty. He graduated from the academy and is now a sergeant in a major city department. He met his future wife, Kelsie, in college and they have been married for four years. Kelsie works in the municipal insurance business as a Member Services Associate. No children yet. Waiting patiently.

Rhonda Willis ~ Senior Photo 1969

Kent and Rhonda ~ 1979 Raimie, Jaimie, and Toby

Kent and Rhonda, Toby, Raimie, Jaimie, Brandie and Dustin

Rai, Victoria, Shannon, Abbi; front row, Dailee and Ryan

Triston, Jennifer, Jaimie, and Kendal

Robyn, Toby Jr., Toby Sr., and Tyler

Brandie "The Princess"

Wedding: Dustin, Rai, Brandie, Jaimie, and Toby

Rusty, Brandie and Ryder

Kelsie and Dustin Wedding Day

Kelsie and Dustin

Kent and Rhonda

CHAPTER THIRTEEN
~Kent and I Started Anew, Again~

After Kent was offered the new job in Tulsa, Oklahoma, we found our life in a new community, Verdigris, as mentioned before. We faced many new challenges. We started attending a church in town, but we did not feel it was a good fit. We church shopped and found one that was a better fit for us at the time. Our new church was very big on small groups. We did find some new friends, but none were as close as the group we were with when we first married. Lacking that support, we felt isolated and it seemed we were only involved with people who were involved in our kids' sports. This made life difficult at times. One does not share your heart and life with people on the bleachers. So, the result was when the kids were grown and married and had their own children, we felt isolated. We realized we had very few friends. Kent had developed some friendships with co-workers and my co-coach, SuzAnn, was my closest friend here. We were almost attached at the hip for fifteen years. Kent and I have grandkids now that are involved in sports, so we are part of the bleacher crowd again. We moved in 1993 to Oklahoma and it is now 2020.

In 2001, I was injured catching a cheerleader falling out of a stunt. She came down very fast and straight to me. I was the only thing keeping her from a serious injury. Stepping under her, I grabbed her and pulled her down on top of me. She was fine. Thank Goodness! Something popped in my back and there was horrible pain. Continuing the practice, I hoped to walk it off. The rest of the summer was full of coaching and I had been selected as the East All-State coach that year. This is a once-in-a-career honor and I needed to coach the girls at the all-state games at the end of July. I did not want to miss this honor. In August, I went to the doctor and found out I had herniated three disks. I was given a shot to help with the pain. It did help, and I started going to a chiropractor which eased the pain enough that I could function. As time went on, I began having some real rough times. The pain was increasing, and it hurt to walk, sit, or stand. I was still teaching and coaching. Dustin was in high school. By this time my mother was living with us and my husband was still travelling for his job. Finally, I had to give up and have surgery. In October of 2003, the surgery consisted of using mesh and placing the disks back in place. It was fixed for the time being, but I was told that I would need surgery again, in the future. The next surgery would be major. It would entail screws and plates and a much longer recovery time.

For a while, my life was almost normal. Sometimes the back would ache, but I was pretty sure it was weather related. I was good at predicting snow and rain! Knowing at some point, I would need another surgery, my aim was to put it off for as long as possible. I was just fifty-two and otherwise in good health. With the aid of chiropractic visits to deal with my neck and upper back, I managed to squeak out eleven years before the next surgery was needed. The next surgery was to address the lower back injury from before. I decided it was time. Knowing this was going to be a big one, I began to plan for a full six weeks off. The surgery went well, and I felt much better, for a while.

By this time, we had found a church as was mentioned before. Our son was now becoming a lay speaker at the church we attended. We still attended the blue jean service and it had gotten so big that we had to meet in the sanctuary. This took away the relaxed feeling of the round tables and chairs. Kent did not feel as relaxed in this service. Since he was on the road, I continued to attend church. I became part of one of the lady's circles. I still was coaching, but my mother and mother-in-law who had been in a nursing home nearby had passed away. Basically, I was an empty nester. At one time or another the kids had moved back, when their lives were in transition. Building a new house, moving back to Oklahoma, were just two of the reasons. Some stayed over a year. Some stayed much less time. I enjoyed the company and we were glad to help. It also allowed us to become closer with the grandkids. Kent was able to come back about twice a month, when the job permitted. When in Denver, he flew home every weekend. In Pennsylvania, Louisiana, Wyoming, and Utah, he tried to get back once a month but sometimes it was six weeks. Anytime we had a break at school, I travelled to visit him. I enjoyed meeting the people he worked with and we saw some wonderful country together. The Pocono Mountains, the Great Salt Lake, Carlsbad National Park, Chaco Canyon National Park, Mesa Verde, Yellowstone, the Rocky Mountains National Park, Royal Gorge, and Roswell were just a few of the great places we visited. Even though we were having wonderful times, I could not wait for us to be able to retire and be together. After our retirement our first big trip on the list was New England in the fall. We were lucky because Kent has a fifth wheel for his field jobs, so we could travel at our leisure. We couldn't wait to see New Hampshire and Vermont and their fall colors. We hoped to be able to come back for as many of our grandkids' games and activities as we could. It will be a great life. Not quite there yet though. Vacations have always been important to us.

There are several vacations I remember, but one of my favorites was going to San Francisco to see my cousin. My dad, the youngest in his family, was more like a brother to Bud. Flying was out of the question, but a road trip was in order. My Uncle Forrest was Bud's dad and he went along with us. Mom, Dad, Uncle Forrest, and I headed West. It was a long ride for a six-year old, but Uncle Forrest's love of history made the geography come alive. The Plains, the Rocky Mountains, the Mojave Desert, The Redwood Forest, and the Coast was all explained to me in colorful detail. I loved it. As a matter of fact, it was this trip that helped create my love of history and geography.

One trip Kent, Brandie, Dustin and I took that really changed our view of the U.S. was when we went back East. We were going to pick up one of the kids in New Jersey. We always tried to have family time every year by going on a vacation together. We chose the Branson area for about thirty years, but this was a new opportunity to see a different part of the country. This trip really changed Kent's perspective of several states including upstate New York, Pennsylvania and New Jersey. He had thought everything east of Ohio was New York City. Neither of us had realized there were large areas of farming and very rural communities for miles and miles.

We had rented a two-story house in the Pocono Mountains for a week. The land was so beautiful. A huge mountain lake was on the property, as well as stables and a large swimming pool. We could have spent a lot of time there, but we wanted to spread our wings a bit and go on daily excursions. This part of the country has such a rich history. We wanted to see as many historical sites as possible. We went to forts, where Washington crossed the Delaware River and then marched on to Trenton. We were able to see where this battle took place and the rugged terrain that had to be crossed to get to Trenton. The highest points in each state were visited. Some of the views were indescribable. One of the most impressive areas was Gettysburg. The size of the battlefield was much bigger than I had imagined. We were offered a private tour that was well worth our time. It helped to really understand what happened there so long ago. Many lives were forever touched by this battle. It was possible to stand in the same spot where President Lincoln gave the Gettysburg Address.

We also made a day trip to Westerly, Rhode Island and went to a nearby beach. We found the beach and ocean to be a lot cleaner than those areas further south. This really began to help me see that my own little world was quite small. People all over live differently, but we all have basic needs and we all have a journey to travel. We all have a story to tell and these should be shared when possible. Travel truly opens our eyes and hearts to others. Every family should travel and spend a week or two on the road.

CHAPTER FOURTEEN
~Back to the Real World~

As mentioned earlier, my second back surgery had been a success, or so I believed. The one thing I did not expect was that the surgery changed my gait. I did not walk with a limp, but I did walk much slower. Gradually pain started to develop in my leg, specifically in my groin. It was nerve pain. If you have experienced it, you know it limits one's mobility. It progressively became worse. I prayed for the pain to go away. I still did not have time for this. Coaching, teaching, being a wife, mom, and grandma kept me busy. Over the years I had learned to do a lot of things at once. The one thing I didn't work into my schedule well was me time. I decided I had to do something. I made an appointment with my primary care doctor and he sent me to a specialist. Many X-rays and tests later, I was told BOTH hips were bone on bone. How could I be so lucky? I told myself I had to figure out a time that I could have two surgeries. Yes, both hips needed a total replacement. I would have to be off at least 12 weeks in the next year. Thank goodness it would not be consecutively.

I had to slow down. I had been on the state cheer board twenty years. Two of these years were as an advisor. I loved what I was doing but I had to get rid of this pain. The doctor decided it would be best to get one replacement done in July and the second one would follow about three months later. Was there a reason why God was forcing me to slow down? Lord knows I would not have done it on my own. Through prayer I felt I needed to write my story. Physically, I could not do what I had been doing anymore. The pain was way too intense.

I began to think about an article for a faith magazine. I realized there was too much to tell for that. I had a couple of stories published in a faith- based magazine our church distributed four times a year. One was about being with my dear mom when she passed away. It was a very tender moment. The nurses had told me she was very close to passing. Our son Jaimie was there and prayed with us. Holding her hand, I watched as she took shallow breaths and I could see her face relaxing and her breathing had begun to slow. Being able to say goodbye and tell her I loved her was very hard. She seemed so at peace. Now, I had another story to tell. Since I had my first exposure to writing for others to read, I knew this story was a much bigger undertaking. As I prayed, I felt a need to put together my life in such a way that readers could see how God had worked to bring me to my purpose. I had thought my purpose was to follow my heart. I was nine years old when I felt God had told me my reason for being born. Or had he? I am beginning to believe my experiences were not accidental but a plan to bring me to the point of this book. He shows you, if one is willing, God will truly bring into your life the good and the bad to share. It is part of the human experience. We truly do not exist as an island. Our SOULS bind us together. Our experiences are not to be hidden. It does not matter what your faith is. We are all connected. We truly need each other.

At one point in my later sixties, when I awakened, I felt I had to write. God had placed this on my heart. Sometimes my writing is not actually putting words on paper. Sometimes it is praying. Sometimes it is just thinking. But again, a song made me understand what I am to do. "The River" sung by Garth Brooks. After these words began to sink in, I knew what I had to do. I knew just because I had spent forty-four years teaching and coaching, I was not finished. I had more to do. I had been lucky because I knew my purpose at a young age, but now what? Writing began to dominate my thoughts and exactly how was I supposed to accomplish this. I had never attempted this size of a project before. Even if I retired, I knew I would still be busy. The two hip replacements were done and at first seemed to work. But soon the right hip became just as painful as it had been before the replacement. This was the final straw that helped me make the decision to retire. I felt a bit lost, but could not deal with it anymore. The pain continued and after about a year and a half, the source of the pain was located. My appliance was extremely loose to the point of becoming separated. Because it was moving around so much it was difficult to determine on an X-ray. Finally, we had something to try to help the pain. Surgery was scheduled, and I waited. While waiting I started writing. I had to take it easy, so I decided to make the most of it. Thus, this book was started. Working daily on it was not necessarily putting words on the page. Praying became a much bigger part of my life. Sometimes I would just clear my mind through prayer and ask for words to go on the page that would be helpful to others. Soon I began to realize even the super-rich, super-gifted, as well as the poor and what appeared to be the most damaged people in the world, all have a story. No one's life is perfect. Sometimes we forget that. One should always be kind to others because you never know what those you encounter are going through.

The second surgery on my right hip was a success. The failing appliance was taken out and a new one put in. It was then screwed in place. This time it would be almost impossible for it to come apart. The next three months were a dream come true. No pain. I could stop taking all the pills. Gradually, my body began to respond like it should. Everyone told me that they could tell immediately when they saw me that my pain was gone. I thought it was the way I moved. The response was, yes, but that was not all. My friends said my whole face was different. My countenance was softer. My eyes were not filled with pain. I did not realize the pain had not only changed my appearance, but my personality as well. After a couple of weeks, I felt so good, I had energy to spare. I began walking in the stores rather than riding a scooter. Finally, I felt myself coming back. I began to question my choices. "Should I have left the career I loved? Should I go back to teaching?" Kent was working in Tulsa now and didn't feel he would have to go out in the field. I went so far as to call my school and thought about working part- time, maybe subbing, or contributing in some way. I talked to our school counselor and my former principal. They encouraged me and I was very close to going to school and making a commitment. Still working on my book, I suddenly was being sidetracked again. I started thinking in terms of maybe doing some other career. After all I have a Masters' degree, somebody would surely want someone such as me to work for them. I started thinking about what I could do. Maybe I could be a greeter or something, anything to help others. My love for people and books might lead to a job at a bookstore. Brick-and-mortar bookstores are coming back, because not everyone likes to read books on an electronic device. I myself like to hold a book and I love the smell of a bookstore. Other ideas started flooding my mind.

I was not working much on this project. We recently had

a wonderful vacation with the family. I was totally ready to start a new job. I did feel a little guilty that I was not writing. I started putting it off. Kent was working and I became bored being by myself so much. We had discussed his retiring too. It was very scary because we had a good life and didn't know what it would be like without a paycheck coming every week. Our retirement and 401k should take care of us fine, but to step out in faith that God will take care of us was hard. He has taken care of us for forty years. Why would he stop now? So, should I start a new job? Should he retire and get a side job? We could be busy visiting our families that we haven't seen in a long time. We could enjoy watching our grandkids and their sports. There are cheerleading events to go see, football games, basketball games, baseball games etc., As quickly as my mind was searching for something to do, my immediate future was limited again.

The morning started as every other morning. I was enjoying my coffee and breakfast bar. The shower was calling my name, so I decided to shower and get dressed. I put my clothes for the day on my bed and entered the shower. After washing my hair, I put the conditioner on and washed myself as I waited for the conditioner to do its magic. As I turned around to rinse the conditioner out, my hip that had given me NO problems for twenty-one months suddenly dislocated. My left hip, the one I had worked extra hard because the other was still a little weak, knocked my good leg out from under me. On the shower floor, my left hip locked out of joint and there was no way to put weight on it. My phone was on the nightstand in the bedroom. On the shower floor with hot water pelting me, I could not reach the faucet. So, I decided I was going to have to belly crawl out to get to the phone.

Luckily our shower is separate from our tub. Getting out of the shower was difficult but I made it. I spent most of the army-crawl cheering myself on to get to the phone. The phone was about thirty feet away. What seemed like forever was realistically about five minutes. I called my husband first and then dialed 911. I grabbed a robe from my bottom drawer of the dresser and covered myself as best I could. My husband called our son and he in turn called my grandson. Thankfully they arrived at the house first. We have locks on the door that use codes. Thank goodness they did not have to break the door down. Jaimie brought me a bigger robe that got me totally covered. The firetruck, ambulance, and police arrived just behind them. Kent arrived soon after. I am thankful I was not exposed to the world. Anyway, they got me on a sheet type cot on which the EMTs could carry me downstairs. The stairs have a corner to navigate so it was difficult getting me to the bottom. They really did great and I was not injured any further. The ambulance ride was interesting. I tried to imagine where we were.

Upon arriving at the hospital, I was taken into a treatment room. The doctors looked about the age of my oldest grandson, twenty-one or so. They immediately told me what they needed to do. I would have to be put under for a short time and they were going to relocate my hip. They chased the family out. They later said I went under very easily. It did not seem to have taken too long. The only problem was I stopped breathing. Even though I was out, they would tell me to breathe in and out and I followed instructions. After I came to, I had to wait a little while and they sent me back home. I had to follow up with my surgeon and I was told to take it easy. No more walking eight to ten thousand steps per day. A week and a half later, I visited my doctor and he, as I, could not understand why it dislocated. I was praying it would not happen again. It had been about two weeks and so far, so good. My tailbone was very sore and I learned I must keep my phone as close as possible. Someday, it will be a funny story. Too soon right now though. Because of this injury, I decided that I should get back to writing this book. I wonder if God was making a point. I shouldn't be surprised. I needed a push to get back to writing.

Right before the injury, we had gone to Kent's 50th class reunion. So many of his friends were gone. They had died from everything from heart attacks to cancer. The same week of the dislocation, a very dear friend passed away. Janet had taken care of me following my surgeries. It was so unexpected. It caused us to start rethinking retirement. I had been working since I was fifteen, fifty-two years. Kent had worked since he was twelve, fifty-seven years! We wanted to live life as we wanted for a change. After much discussion we decided in two months we would both be retired. We might pick up odd jobs only if needed. We had everything we could possibly want so we just needed to adjust our standard of living a bit. Life is too precious to let it pass you by. We need to live while we can because someday, in a blink of an eye, our life on earth could be done.

I thought I was fixed for a while. Little did I know that I would be back at the ER two more times within the month. The second dislocation took place at physical therapy. I was doing my exercises and down to the easier part of the therapy. The therapist was stretching my legs a bit and boom. Out it went. I was laying on my back on a table. What happened? An ambulance arrived and off to the hospital again. After three or four hours I was on my way back home. Things went great the next few days and I had a big football/cheer reunion coming up. I asked one of the nurses in my doctor's office if I could go. She said yes but be careful. I wore my brace all week. I was feeling great and was looking forward to the re-union.

I prayed diligently that I could go to the reunion without yet another dislocation happening. This was a special football game. Fifty years ago, my high school put our first ever football team on the field. It was also the first time the cheerleaders ever cheered for football. There were twenty-four football players and four cheerleaders who made it to the reunion. It was a fun-filled two days. I enjoyed the visiting and reconnecting with my high school friends. I had not seen many of them since graduation. We returned from the reunion on Saturday evening. Sunday morning, we readied ourselves for church. I was feeling great and was armed with pictures from the game. I couldn't wait to share them. I greeted and spoke to everyone as they came into the sanctuary. It was Communion Sunday and there would be a full house. As usual, I had picked up a water on the way to my seat.

I had thought the most embarrassing thing that could have happened to me was my hip dislocating in the shower. Church was about to begin, and I took one last sip of my water. I leaned a little to the right to set down my bottle. "Pop, Kerplunk," there it went again. Pain travelled from my hip to my foot. I tried to stay very still. If I did not move, maybe the pain would be minimal. Everyone sprung to action, 911 was called, the chairs were moved back out of the way so the EMTs could get to me. The side door was opened, and the ambulance crew came rushing inside. At first the EMTs tried to just lift me on the gurney. Nope, wouldn't work. Pain shot through my entire body. The ambulance did not have any medications to curb the pain. One of the EMTs grabbed a sheet and slipped it under me and on the count of three they lifted. It worked. I was loaded into the ambulance with minimal pain. We were off again to the ER. Did I mention the pastor of our church is our son? My husband had decided to retire early after my second dislocation. Our kids had a surprise retirement party after church around 2:00 PM planned for him.

The next few hours I was fighting the pain. Still no meds. I asked for something to take the edge off and they said okay. About that time someone came in who was yelling loudly. Everyone rushed to help him. So, I waited. A team was assembled and they put me back together. It was about 2:45 PM. Our daughter was with us and I told Kent we needed to take her to Toby's house where his retirement party was being held. Made it just an hour and fifteen minutes late. Who says I can't multi-task? I needed another surgery to fix the first surgery on my left hip. They went in and fixed it making it impossible for it to dislocate again. After seventeen months, so far, so good.

CHAPTER FIFTEEN
~Is it over Yet~

I totally hoped all the surgeries were done. So far, I had an ankle replaced, two back surgeries and four, yes four hip surgeries. All these had surely fixed my problems. Remember all of this started from catching a cheerleader that was going to be hurt badly if I had not caught her. I started having pains in my left shoulder. I thought it would get better but as time passed, I found out I was mistaken. I had spent five years lifting myself up from a sitting position by pushing with my arms. My left arm ached and sometimes Aleve would help it but other times, it would not. It started to affect my sleep. I could not sleep on my left side which was my favorite position. It was hard to sleep on my back. It would start aching after a few minutes. My right hip was the one that had come apart, so I did not want to risk that again. My left side, pillow between my knees, left arm straight out and head on a pillow was the only possible position. It was not the most comfortable, but I could sleep a little.

Finally, I decided to visit my Orthopedic Surgeon's office that had done my hip replacements. He referred me to a shoulder surgeon. As I spoke to him, he decided to get an x-ray. After seeing it, he decided an MRI was in order. The MRI was scheduled, and I prayed it would be ok.

It was not good news. We found out that the rotator cuff was torn and the bones in my shoulder were bone on bone. He said I needed a total shoulder replacement. I was becoming the bionic woman. He said I could decide when I wanted the surgery. It would not make his job any harder. How much pain could I handle? I do not like to take pain medications. I put off the surgery two times, but decided I was going to have to have it to move on with my life. It is such a hard decision because I will be grounded for six weeks maybe more. I will be so restricted in my activity and I will have physical therapy for six weeks. Oh well, jumping in with both feet is my style. And here we go again. The next thing I realize it is March 2020. I had planned a surgery at the end of that month. Covid-19 put a stop to all elective surgeries. Besides, being in the hospital environment would not be great for me. I am nearly seventy and have a greater risk of getting ill. Again the surgery was postponed. Someday when life becomes a little safer, I will need to get this done. So, in the meantime, I continued working on the book.

Life is so full of ups and downs. Sometimes one wants to just give up and say; "Whatever". But then something changes and hope creeps back again. I recall being told by many of my elders that time will fix everything. At the time, I felt they did not have a clue about how bad things were. Everyone understands to one extent or another. They might not have the same experiences, but you can bet they have their own battles to fight. No matter how they look on the outside, after time, hopefully each person will be able to look back and see how God was the architect of their life. We each have our own experiences, and sometimes I have learned that sharing with others the story can be soul cleansing for self but also helps others realize they too can work through the bad. It is true. It is all attitude. No matter the circumstance, you are capable of willing yourself to be joyful. I remember once when I was really experiencing circumstances that seemed overwhelming, one of my fellow teachers told me she knew I was going through a rough time but was amazed that I always seemed to have a good word and smile for people. That smile was a deliberate choice and I chose joy for those days. Sometimes you must say "no" to depression. That does not mean that depression is not real. People just handle it in different ways. Faith and praise for some work. Our nation is full of mental illness and people need to understand that it is no different than any other illness. The stigma needs to go away. Seek help. Everyone processes grief differently. It does not mean one is weak if they cannot fix it on their own.

Joy is not a given. It always helps to have friends you can share life with. Sometimes that is all that is needed. For others it is a situation in which only a professional's help will do. Turning to drugs or alcohol is only a temporary fix and could possibly lead down a path of helplessness. Hope sometimes seems evasive but, one must just cling to it.

CHAPTER SIXTEEN
~THE KIDS~

Remembering my childhood dream of a large family, I think about the naïve life I had as a child. Not totally understanding what it took to raise a big family, I learned things daily. Little boys and our one little girl had great imaginations. I wasn't quite prepared for that aspect of raising children. Life went into overdrive. Out of necessity, I learned quickly to expect the unexpected. As all families, we have favorite stories about each child. Raising five kids was exciting and challenging at the same time. One thing I did not share about the kids was the fact, like their dad, they were ADD. We are very proud of their successes in life and will share later about what worked for us and them. As you might suspect, each one was different. Growing up in small Missouri towns, we have collected several stories starring each child. The following stories are only some of the ones we treasure. Enjoy.

Rai was the oldest in our newly formed family. He was the most outspoken and we could always find him in a crowded loud gym because he was always the loudest kid there. He was such a sweet and boisterous child. I found out soon that he was very afraid of strange dogs. One day walking home he was attacked by a big dog that tore his coat to pieces. Obviously, it scared him to death. After a while he began to realize it was fine. Luckily his coat saved him from injury and on the bright side, he did get a new coat. He was fine around our dogs but did not want anything to do with strange ones. He now has a love of dogs of all sizes, mostly big ones.

One day he decided to ride his three-year-old brother's

big wheel. Not a good choice. He came barreling down the small mountain to the side and front of our house. He spun out and crashed. He flipped the big wheel. He had what looked like a huge cut on his head. He came running in the house screaming. By looking at him and all the blood, I knew he was going to need stitches. I grabbed a washcloth and began to slowly clean the wound. What I found was a small puncture wound. I did not feel he needed an emergency room visit after all. He, however, was not so sure. Once he calmed down, I finally convinced him he was fine, and a band-aid would fix it. Band-aid in place, outside he went. Crisis averted. Not funny at the time but now, yes.

Another time we were at an amusement park. We rode a ride called Ed Doogin's Diving Bell. It was done in such a way, that one felt like the small submarine went down into the lake. As we cruised under water, suddenly, another submarine came racing toward our sub and ended up crashing into us. Water appeared to be flowing in and we were sure to sink. We tried to tell the kids it was just a ride and we were not really sinking. We were in no danger. Rai was about eight and he was having no part of it. The next thing we knew all three of our kids were screaming and every child on the sub ride knew our lives were over. The parents were trying to settle their kids. We couldn't help but laugh when the door slid open and the kids could see we had never moved from the dock. Not too long after our horrifying experience, the sub ride was gone. Hope it wasn't us. Maybe the ride was a little ahead of its time?

At our house in Newburg in the early 80s, we had a large fenced-in back yard. Kent came home from work one evening as I was cooking dinner getting ready for his arrival.

He did not even say hello but came rushing through the house to the back yard. I turned off the stove and followed him through to the screened-in porch and saw smoke billowing from the side of the house. I could not even understand what was taking place at first. I thought the house was on fire. Kent had a hose and was spraying it at the corner of the house. It was not the house thank goodness but a bush that was by the house. Kent quickly extinguished the fire. All we could get from the kids was it was a total accident. It had begun to spread to the rest of the back yard. If Kent had not arrived when he did, I hate to think what might have happened.

Our house also had a crawl space that was under half the house. It was on the front side. The other side had a basement. The kids played under there and it was like their fort. The space was about four feet high. The floor was dirt. So, what could they possibly hurt? One day I was upstairs cleaning up and the three boys were under the house playing. The neighbor boys were with them. Suddenly, I smelled smoke. I could not find where it was coming from. The kids could evidently hear me running through the house above and started giggling. I heard the giggles and realized the smoke smell had to be coming from under the house. I ran outside and went to the crawl space and sure enough the boys had decided to build a campfire under the house. There is some argument as to whose idea it was, but Rai ended up being chosen. Matches are a mom's enemy. Wow, now one might think this kid was always up to mischief, but it could not be further from the truth. He also was a good helper and a very loving little boy. His smile would lighten up the room. I prayed every day that God would watch after our family and help me help Kent to raise these boys. As time went on, I became a little more

94

knowledgeable of what creative little boys could conjure up in their minds for excitement.

When we moved from Newburg and lived along the Meramec River, the two older boys spent a lot of time at the river. We also had about five acres in which to play and run. We had acquired a minibike. It was really a little small for Rai, but he of course had to ride it. The boys decided to build a ramp. They became in their minds, at least, Evil Kinevil. Several jumps were made and Rai was ready to give it a try. He backed it up legs dragging and headed for the ramp. He got air and sailed into the jump. As he became airborne, the front wheel came flying off the minibike. When he landed, the front fork planted itself in the ground sending him over the handlebars sprawling. Luckily, again he was not hurt but it was sure a funny sight. Just about anytime we are all get together this story comes up. Rai has always had a great heart. He also has proven himself as a valuable leader in his job in the army as well as now in his civilian job. He could make someone sooooo mad but then on a dime, turn the situation around. He sometimes tested my patience, but we are so proud of the man, husband and father he has become. He certainly is and continues to be a product of prayer. Rai and Shannon have been married twenty-three years and they have Tori, Abbi, Ryan, and Dailee.

Jaimie was a smart little boy and he learned how to manipulate people at a very young age. He says he was shy. I didn't see him as shy, but very observant. He knew exactly what buttons to push to make someone feel awful or when he wanted something, he could wrap an unsuspecting person around his little finger. He had big sad brown eyes that could melt a heart or shoot daggers.

Jaimie was in love with his kindergarten teacher. He would intentionally act up in class so he could spend time alone with his teacher at recess when he was not allowed to go out to play. This was only on days his teacher did not have playground duty. Sly and creative little Romeo.

There was another time he was banished to his room. I found out later that he had opened the window in his room and was moaning and groaning so the whole neighborhood could hear every dramatic noise. The neighbors would without a doubt be sympathetic to this poor little boy undergoing such horrible punishment. Jaimie was famous for being sent to his room and when we told him he could come out, he would reply, "No I'm fine."

Jaimie was always Rai's guinea pig. If Rai was unsure about whether something would work or not, he would have Jaimie give it a try. Then if Jaimie made it, then and only then would he try. Another time Jaimie and Rai were wrestling (fighting), and Jaimie jumped on Rai's shoulders. Rai immediately threw Jaimie off and as Jaimie fell off backwards Rai's ear lobe was caught between Jaimie's big toe and second toe. It ripped Rai's ear from his head about an inch from the bottom. I gathered up the kids and headed to the ER. I called Kent to meet us there. He had to have stitches to repair the ear. Try explaining this to ER doctors and Kent. Consequently, when you hear a story that sounds impossible, little boys can accomplish the most unlikely scenarios.

Another Jaimie story that shows the determination of this young boy, is the Mississippi River and Missouri River heated discussion on the way to school. Jaimie was in third grade and we were discussing the geography of our state. Since we lived in a river town, the discussion shifted to rivers of Missouri. Jaimie began to discuss the Mississippi and how it ran between basically Kansas City and St. Louis. I said, "No Jaimie it runs along the Eastern border of Missouri." Jaimie answered, "No the Missouri River runs down the Eastern side of Missouri." We went back and forth for the next three blocks and he was not giving an inch. He insisted that I go to his classroom so he could show me on the map. We walked in the room and went straight to the Missouri map. He proudly and with confidence pointed to the map and said, "See!" I, as a geography teacher, had to point out on the map that he had the two confused. He turned to me with complete confidence and a straight face with brown eyes a blazing, "The map is wrong!!" To this day when someone has their information wrong and need correction, the reply is always, "Is this going to be another Missouri River/ Mississippi River debate?

We had decided to take the boys on a camping trip to Branson. We also planned to go to Silver Dollar City and to see The Shepherd of the Hills Play. We put up our tents at the Shepherd of the Hills campground. It was a beautiful campsite. After a long day of swimming and just enjoying the outdoors, we were very tired and ready to hit the sleeping bags. The two older boys had put up their own two-man tent haphazardly, and Kent, Toby, and I had put up a bigger dome tent. As we all settled in listening to the tree frogs and dozing off, a whip-poor-will decided on a concert. After about two minutes of its song, Jaimie yelled loud enough for the campground to hear, "SHUT UP, SHUT UP, SHUT UP." It didn't shut up and continued, then we hear a very disgusted Jaimie say, "Great, just great." We looked out of our tent window and saw their tent had completely collapsed. They did not try to fix it and they slept under their tent. It was safe and evidently comfy. We heard their snores later. To this day Jaimie loves listening to birds singing just NOT a whip-poor-will. Jaimie and Jennifer have been married twenty- three years and have a boy and girl, Triston and Kendal.

Toby was the quiet one of the three older boys. This was because he did not need to speak. The older boys would speak for him. "Toby's hungry." Why bother? He could not get a word in edgewise. It wasn't he couldn't talk because when he started to speak, he spoke in sentences right off the bat. He loved wrestling with Dad as all the kids did and I can still hear him saying, "Come on les ge him," as one of his first sentences. He liked taking things apart and "fixing" things like his dad did. He was involved in sports too. Now three boys to take to soccer practices etc. Our life was very busy.

Toby was a child that when it was bedtime, he went to sleep, no matter where he might be. One night at a scout meeting his bedtime came and "kerplunk," he fell off the chair onto the floor. He did not wake up, he just continued to sleep on the floor. Another time, he was sent to the corner and the next thing I knew, he was asleep. I went to check on him, he was in the corner with his gym shorts around his ankles snoring. One of the funniest Toby stories was after he was all grown up and we were in Oklahoma in our new home. Kent and I had gone back to Missouri for a quick trip and Toby, Jaimie, and Dustin were at home. We called home to check on things and heard screaming and yelling in the background. Dustin had answered the phone and I asked to talk to one of the older boys. He said they were busy trying to catch a squirrel. What? How did a squirrel get in the house? Dustin replied, "through the toilet." The funny part is Toby was on the toilet at the time. Wow, I can't imagine. Anyway, we called as they were trying to catch it with a blanket. A scared, wet and mad baby squirrel is capable of totally messing up a bathroom and wherever else he might run. Finally, the three guys were successful, and the squirrel was thrown outside safe and sound. Baby squirrel was off into the night to find his way back home. After much discussion, we found out how the squirrel got in the toilet. There is a vent pipe on the top of the house that hooks up with the toilet. The little squirrel must have fallen down the pipe and fought his way through the water and tried to escape the toilet bowl. He was swimming toward the light until it had been put out by Toby. So, trying to preserve his little squirrel life, he plunged forward trying to burst through the darkness.

Another time we were in Missouri and called home to Oklahoma and the fire alarm was going off. Again, what had happened? A towel used to block air from coming in around the fireplace insert had caught fire. Toby and Jaimie had decided to build a fire. They had forgotten about the towel. We were not far from home, so we sped up and were immediately pulled over by a highway patrolman. We tried to tell him our house was on fire, but he said the judge could make that decision. Oh well sometimes you shouldn't leave even adult children at home.

After many years working in the construction industry, Toby now works as a construction superintendent running big jobs for a major construction company. He is totally enjoying his work and is very good at it. He has done remodels of many hospitals and other large projects. He and Robyn have been married twenty-two years and they have two sons, Toby Jr. and Tyler.

Brandie, our delicate little flower, did not stay this way for long. She had to live with three brothers from the very beginning, and eventually four. She became a good athlete and held her own. She was more outgoing than the others and when we moved to Oklahoma, she stood at the door her first day of school handing out her phone number. And, as I have mentioned, she was always very competitive. On a family vacation and a particularly heated Scrabble game, she went down arguing for a word. It was in a song so how could it not be a word? The word was EIEIO. This is still a word we refer to when she is arguing a losing battle. Not often, but it does come up periodically.

Brandie had built-in bodyguards. Everyone who has kids knows that siblings can fight like cats and dogs but woe be it to anyone who says anything bad about their sister or brother. One time when Brandie was in junior high, some guy in a neighboring town said some bad things about her. He didn't even know her, and she did not know him. Two of the boys, Toby and Jaimie, went to a local hangout and found him. Rai was overseas at the time. Toby confronted him and said, "You better quit talking about my sister." "So," the young man said. He was trying to be all tough. Then Jaimie stepped out of the car and said I am her brother too. He did heed the warning, and never bothered or spoke badly of her again. Can you imagine if all four had shown up ranging from five feet ten inches to six feet five? The boys became well known and they intimidated a lot of young suitors.

One time we were all home and Brandie had a boyfriend over. Rai said to him, "Get me a glass of tea," and he immediately stood up and got him the tea. Rai was pulling his chain. Remember, dad is six foot four inches, and 230 lbs.

Lots of interesting times. They were all so protective. One time all the kids and Kent were at the gym and were playing pick-up basketball games. Our kids were on a team playing against people who would challenge them. The challengers did not realize four were or had been college basketball players. One person on the team had to guard the girl. No one wanted to guard her because they wanted more of a challenge. So, as her matchup complained about guarding her the game started. First three trips down the floor the boys passed to Brandie and swish, three, three- pointers to start the game. The person that was guarding her could not stop her. He said, "Could someone please guard the girl?" Our team won! Brandie and Rusty have been married eleven years and have one son, Ryder.

Our youngest was also quiet. Dustin was four years younger than Brandie so when they were smaller, he was a tag-along. He also thought he was as big as the older boys so he would try anything he saw them do. The boys were play-ing timber. Timber is a game that you stand and drop down to a pushup position, yelling "TIMBER." Great fun for older children but Dustin was eighteen months old. He was standing on a chair and yelled "Timbuh," and he tried to catch himself when he hit the floor. He let out a huge scream and started crying hysterically. I ran in and found the older boys trying to help him up. His arm did not look right. I gathered him up and headed to the doctor. He had what they called a green-stick fracture. So, he was put in a cast. A greenstick fracture can result in young children. The bone is still not rigid, and it bends instead of breaking. Dustin was perpetual motion. He always played hard and seemed to never tire. He would be outside all the time and after we bought a trampoline, he could be seen jumping on it for hours.

We started noticing our rods on our blinds were disappearing. We finally understood what was happening. Our creative little boy was using them for swords. He was jumping on the trampoline and fighting his enemies. He was totally consumed by this activity. One day I asked him what he was doing on the trampoline when he came in. He looked straight at me with his big hazel eyes and said seriously, "I am fighting the Badsters." I thought he was trying to say something else, so I asked what he meant. He said, "the bad guys." Oh, that made sense and low and behold, he still is fighting the badsters.

There are some kids who just aren't good liars. He could not do anything against the rules, or he would get caught. He just did not have it in him. After a few attempts, he decided it was easier just to be honest. It has served him well. He is very much trusted by all that know him. Once when a friend of ours was asked about him for a job application, she answered, "Put it this way, I wish he would marry my daughter." He was also considered a great lifeguard by his bosses. Dustin met Kelsie in college, and they have been married over four years. They love hiking and camping. He and Kelsie adopted a fur baby and seem very happy with life. Dustin is a Police Sergeant in a major city. No kids yet, but we are patiently waiting for our nine grandchildren to become ten.

As one can see, we are very proud of our kids. They all have Christian families and have done quite well for themselves. They are all hard workers and have made a contribution to our society. They are good people. What more could a parent ask?

CHAPTER SEVENTEEN
~STEPS~

Remember, I started my journey young. I knew early I had a purpose and God had a plan for me. It was not to be easy. It caught me off guard and I did not understand. I was willing, but I was not ready. God knew this. I had more living to do before I could possibly be successful in his plan. Now, I look back and see the reason for every twist and turn, every heartache and joy. Everything is in His time and when He feels you are the most prepared for the next step, He will act. Love is patient. Not only God's love is patient with us, we must be patient and trusting to wait until He feels we are ready to move forward. From one person to a family built by God, now we are twenty-one strong and will surely keep growing.

In our society, so many families end up in turmoil and feel a divorce is the only answer. Many times, these breakups lead to new relationships that bring in a step parent. As we don't get parent training, we are not trained to become a step-parent. One must approach it open minded and open hearted. Every circumstance is different. I had never been a parent, so I had no experience whatsoever. I dreamed of becoming a parent, but this was not the dream. I felt I was chosen for this position as I previously discussed. So, how did we make it work? First and foremost, I wanted to do the most I could for the boys. Their biological mom was close for a while but moved away because of her husband's job. The kids saw her once a year. She spoke to them regularly. Their relationship, in my opinion was in their hands. We did not focus on the past.

When the boys asked questions of me, I tried to answer honestly, but carefully chose my words. I told the boys they had two moms and were lucky. The more people to love them the better. We would all do the best we could to be there for them. I told them I did not want to replace her but do the best I could for them. When their bio mom was nearby, we made sure she knew when things were happening like programs etc. When they moved away, I made sure they received the letters she wrote and were able to talk to her anytime she called. Things did not always go perfectly, but we are around each other a lot now since we are both retired and spend time together at games and we consider them friends and part of our family. Our younger kids are used to seeing them around too. We sit together at games and church and any other place we may end up together

Here are my ten tips for raising step-children

1.   Accept who your stepchildren are. Love who they are. The child would not be present without biological parents.

2.   Feel blessed you have a chance to influence a life. Love them and help them as a parent should. Be available for help if needed.

3.   Be a parent without taking the biological parent's place. The children will come to you. They will decide what they want to call you. Let them.

4.   The biological parent is responsible for their relationship with the kids.

5.   Always share important dates and times. Examples will be like Birthday parties, barbeques, and other times family units get together.

6.   Visits to biological parents are a good time to regroup and make upgrades in their rooms. Even if it is just a good cleaning. This keeps step-parents busy and a nice welcome home for the kids. With our busy lives, this time is needed.

7.   You simply love and raise these children and do the very best you can. I was chosen to love the kids and their daddy until life ends. When the kids are grown, the grandkids are yet another gift.

8.   Pray daily for your family unit. That means everyone involved with these children and grandchildren. The more love the better.

9.   Grandkids are so precious. The more grandparents the better. When I was little my last grandparent died when I was three. I never had that part of life until I married Kent. His grandparents were still alive. I found out what having grandparents would be like and it was wonderful.

10. There is no place for jealousy. Combat jealousy with a loving heart. The Golden Rule is always appropriate. You do have the power to choose love.

CHAPTER EIGHTTEEN
~WHAT LIFE HAS TAUGHT ME~

It sounds cliché, but I still have to say it. "Life is about loving and letting go." If you made a decision to follow the teachings of Christ, you must let go. Being a planner, letting go of my plans was the very hardest part. Remember, we as Christians are not in control of our destiny. We can place a timeline on our plan, but it won't be as we think unless God's plan is the same as ours. Things will work in God's time. We as Christians must be patient and open. We can plan all we want, but we must wait until the time is right in God's eyes. The result may be different than what we hoped. It may end as we hope but the journey is not at all what we expect.

In God's eyes, we will be used for His Glory as He chooses. We must be willing to let go and not worry about timing. In my case, I waited ten years for the beginning of the family that I had desired as a child. I understand why every heartache was necessary to prepare me for my walk with Him. My heart was broken over and over and it was so hard to understand while I was living the hurt. It was so hard to avoid bitterness and ask why? But my mom used to tell me "Hindsight is 20/20." Now, I understand what that phrase means. Another phrase my Mom used was "Life is what you make it."

When I was growing up, I understood how family and extended family was very important. I had a great Mom and Dad and two brothers. I lived life with aunts, uncles and cousins. My cousins became my best friends. We visited our families on weekends. We had music parties and all the kids played kick the can, hide and seek, and ate all the food everyone brought. We also would just spend Sunday afternoons visiting. Sometimes we would spend weekends with extended family. Times were so different then. Today family members move all over the place. We very seldom ever spend quality time with extended family. I miss that. Some are fortunate and live within a couple of hours but even then, everyone is so busy we feel we don't have time for parents, brothers, sisters, and cousins. We might keep in touch by phone, Facebook, Instagram, other social media and texting, but it is just not the same. We need to look people in the eye and discuss life. We need to discuss hard topics. We need to support each other by laughing together and crying together. We somehow have isolated ourselves. After our kids grew out of sports, we found we had no friends other than parents of other athletes. They, like us, move on to their grandkids' activities. We lose touch even with those friends. Many older people end up very lonely and depressed.

How do we fill this void? Many churches provide Sunday school, small group classes, and promote small groups that contain people of same likes and values. It is very important to be involved in life with others. It is very hard to step out and form such a group. Pray about the situation and perhaps you will have something come to you. A small group can not only help make new friends, but also, help one feel useful. Sometimes when people get older, their purpose seems to fade. Your purpose on Earth may change. It is never nonexistent. Once you feel your purpose has been completed, there will be something new in your life and you feel rejuvenated. Everyone needs the feeling that their life is of importance. Passion causes people to continue to seek ways to make the world a better place. The feeling of purpose helps lengthen our lives and make us happier in general. Who doesn't want a more meaningful life?

We go through very difficult times in our life. We cannot control the difficulty of life and God knows what needs to be done for us to meet our full potential. He will lead you through the good times and the bad. He will give you the strength to navigate this "River" of life. You are a vessel of God's plan. God says to love and help one another. He does not say love one another only if they are your same color, same religion, same language, or same political belief. Love each other. Life is but a "Dance" and when you come into full meaning, you understand that every step, good and bad, were necessary for you to reach your potential. Hopefully, life on earth will end with no regrets. What a wonderful transition it will be. Live each day fully ...

~'Til the River Runs Dry~

Family Picture missing Kelsie, Triston and Dailee